LIESELLE'S
ETERNAL TAROT

Lieselle Elliot
illustrated by **Sean Frosali**

Copyright © 2025, text by Lieselle Elliot, illustrations by Sean Frosali

Library of Congress Control Number: **2025930154**

All rights reserved. No part of this work may be reproduced or used in any form or by any means—graphic, electronic, or mechanical, including photocopying or information storage and retrieval systems—without written permission from the publisher.

The scanning, uploading, and distribution of this book or any part thereof via the Internet or any other means without the permission of the publisher is illegal and punishable by law. Please purchase only authorized editions and do not participate in or encourage the electronic piracy of copyrighted materials.

"Red Feather Mind Body Spirit" logo is a trademark of Schiffer Publishing, Ltd.
"Red Feather Mind Body Spirit Feather" logo is a registered trademark of Schiffer Publishing, Ltd.

Package design by BMac
Cover design by BMac
Type set in Bernhard Modern/Minion Pro

ISBN: 978-0-7643-6975-9
Printed in China

10 9 8 7 6 5 4 3 2 1

Published by REDFeather Mind, Body, Spirit
An imprint of Schiffer Publishing, Ltd.
4880 Lower Valley Road
Atglen, PA 19310
Phone: (610) 593-1777; Fax: (610) 593-2002
Email: Info@redfeathermbs.com
Web: www.redfeathermbs.com

Trust your voice and then learn to trust the journey

CONTENTS

- 5   Foreword
- 6   A Brief History of the Origins of the Tarot
- 7   Numerology and Its Application in Tarot
- 12   Elements Associated with the Four Suits
- 16   The Major Arcana
- 76   The Minor Arcana
  - 77   The Suit of Wands
  - 114   The Suit of Cups
  - 150   The Suit of Swords
  - 186   The Suit of Pentacles
- 222   Three Tarot Spreads Using *Lieselle's Eternal Tarot*
- 224   Acknowledgments
- 224   Bibliography

FOREWORD

Welcome to *Lieselle's Eternal Tarot*! This special deck is a heartfelt collaboration between my son, Sean Frosali, and me, blending timeless wisdom with stunning contemporary artistry.

Our deck is more than just a collection of cards; it's an invitation to embark on a personal journey of self-discovery. Each card is designed to help you unlock your intuition and delve into the depths of your own wisdom.

Beyond fortune-telling or divination, every card can serve as a guide to deeper insight and personal transformation. We created this deck with the aim of empowering you and nurturing your intuitive abilities.

While our deck pays homage to the traditional Rider-Waite Tarot, it also features beautiful modern artwork meant to inspire and enhance your intuitive journey. We hope it brings you as much joy and insight as it has brought us in creating it. Enjoy your journey!

A BRIEF HISTORY OF THE ORIGINS OF THE TAROT

The Tarot has a rich and intriguing history that spans centuries and continents. Its origins can be traced back to the fifteenth century in Europe, particularly in Italy, where it was initially used as a card game called "tarocchi." These early decks were not primarily intended for divination but as entertainment for the nobility.

The Tarot as we recognize it today began to take shape in the late eighteenth century, when French occultists and mystics such as Jean-Baptiste Alliette (known as Etteilla) and Antoine Court de Gébelin started to ascribe deeper esoteric meanings to the cards. They believed the Tarot was a repository of ancient wisdom and linked it to mystical traditions, such as the Kabbalah and alchemy.

The Rider-Waite-Smith deck, created in 1909 by artist Pamela Colman Smith under the direction of mystic A. E. Waite, marked a significant development in Tarot history. This deck introduced detailed illustrations for the Minor Arcana and became a standard for modern Tarot practice.

Today, the Tarot is widely used for divination, self-reflection, and spiritual guidance, and it continues to evolve with contemporaneous interpretations and artistic expressions.

NUMEROLOGY AND ITS APPLICATION IN TAROT

Numerology is the study of numbers and their mystical significance. Each number carries unique vibrations and meanings that can provide deeper insights into Tarot readings.

The Minor Arcana in this deck is based on the significance of numerology and the elements associated with each suit. Understanding the basic meanings of numbers in numerology can enhance your interpretations of the Tarot cards, offering a more profound and nuanced perspective. Here is a basic outline of the meanings of numbers in numerology and how they apply to the Tarot:

Number One (Ace)

Numerology meaning: Independence, new beginnings, leadership, and initiative

Tarot application: The Ace cards in each suit embody the energy of new beginnings and potential. For example, the Ace of Wands represents a new idea or inspiration, while the Ace of Pentacles symbolizes new financial opportunities or material beginnings.

Number Two (2)

Numerology meaning: Balance, partnership, duality, and harmony

Tarot application: The Two cards reflect themes of partnership and balance. The Two of Cups, for instance, signifies a harmonious union or relationship, while the Two of Swords represents a need for balance and decision-making.

Number Three (3)

Numerology meaning: Creativity, growth, expansion, and communication

Tarot application: The Three cards often indicate growth and creativity. The Three of Pentacles represents collaboration and skill development, while the Three of Cups signifies celebration and social bonds.

Number Four (4)

Numerology meaning: Stability, structure, foundation, and order

Tarot application: The Four cards emphasize stability and structure. The Four of Wands represents a stable home and celebration, while the Four of Pentacles signifies holding on to resources and stability.

Number Five (5)

Numerology meaning: Change, challenge, freedom, and adventure

Tarot application: The Five cards often indicate conflict and change. The Five of Wands represents competition and struggle, while the Five of Pentacles signifies financial hardship and challenges.

Number Six (6)

Numerology meaning: Harmony, responsibility, nurturing, and service

Tarot application: The Six cards reflect themes of harmony and care. The Six of Cups signifies nostalgia and childhood memories, while the Six of Pentacles represents generosity and balance in giving and receiving.

Number Seven (7)

Numerology meaning: Reflection, introspection, spirituality, and wisdom

Tarot application: The Seven cards often indicate introspection and inner growth. The Seven of Swords represents strategy and potential deception, while the Seven of Pentacles signifies reflection on progress and hard work.

Number Eight (8)

Numerology meaning: Power, authority, ambition, and material success

Tarot application: The Eight cards emphasize power and movement. The Eight of Wands represents swift action and communication, while the Eight of Pentacles signifies diligent work and skill mastery.

Number Nine (9)

Numerology meaning: Completion, fulfillment, humanitarianism, and wisdom

Tarot application: The Nine cards often indicate completion and fulfillment. The Nine of Cups represents emotional satisfaction and wishes fulfilled, while the Nine of Swords signifies anxiety and mental challenges.

Number Ten (10)

Numerology meaning: Completion, renewal, transition, and transformation

Tarot application: The Ten cards signify the completion of a cycle and the start of a new one. The Ten of Cups represents ultimate emotional fulfillment, while the Ten of Swords indicates an ending and the potential for new beginnings.

Pages (11)

Numerology meaning: New beginnings, potential, youthfulness, and curiosity

Tarot application: The Pages in each suit represent the start of new phases and the exploration of possibilities, such as emotional exploration with the Page of Cups or practical learning with the Page of Pentacles.

Knights (12)

Numerology meaning: Growth, progress, action, and pursuit

Tarot application: The Knights embody action and movement in their respective suits, such as swift communication with the Knight of Swords or diligent progress with the Knight of Pentacles.

Queens (13)

Numerology meaning: Nurturing, maturity, mastery, and stability

Tarot application: The Queens represent mature, nurturing energy in each suit, such as the confident creativity of the Queen of Wands or practical nurturing with the Queen of Pentacles.

Kings (14)

Numerology meaning: Authority, leadership, mastery, and completion

Tarot application: The Kings symbolize ultimate mastery and authority in their suits, such as the emotional maturity of the King of Cups or the structural power and financial stability of the King of Pentacles.

By understanding the numerological meanings and how they apply to the Tarot, you can enhance your readings and gain deeper insights into the cards' messages. This knowledge helps you see the broader patterns and themes within the Tarot, providing a richer, more nuanced interpretation.

ELEMENTS ASSOCIATED WITH THE FOUR SUITS

Each of the four suits in the Tarot—Wands, Cups, Swords, and Pentacles—is associated with one of the four classical elements: Fire, Water, Air, and Earth. These elements provide a deeper layer of meaning and symbolism to the cards, helping to understand their messages and themes. Here's an outline of the elements associated with each suit and their significance.

Wands: Fire

Element: Fire
Associated qualities: Energy, passion, creativity, action, and ambition

FIRE SYMBOLISM IN TAROT:
   Energy and vitality: Fire represents the spark of life, the energy that fuels action and ambition.
   Passion and desire: Fire is associated with intense emotions, desires, and drive.
   Creativity: The element of Fire is linked to creativity and the pursuit of new ideas and ventures.
   Action and movement: Fire signifies action, movement, and the willingness to take risks.

Themes: Inspiration, creativity, ambition, and spiritual journey

Example cards: Ace of Wands (new inspiration), Three of Wands (expansion and planning), King of Wands (leadership and vision)

Cups: Water

Element: Water
Associated qualities: Emotions, relationships, intuition, compassion, and inner experience

WATER SYMBOLISM IN TAROT:

Emotional depth: Water represents the depth of emotions, highlighting feelings, moods, and emotional responses.

Relationships: Water is associated with connections, love, friendships, and interactions with others.

Intuition: The element of Water is linked to intuition, inner knowing, and psychic abilities.

Compassion and healing: Water signifies compassion, empathy, and the healing of emotional wounds.

Themes: Emotions, relationships, intuition, and inner peace

Example cards: Ace of Cups (new emotional beginnings), Three of Cups (celebration and community), King of Cups (emotional balance and wisdom)

Pentacles: Earth

Element: Earth
Associated qualities: Materiality, stability, practicality, and growth

EARTH SYMBOLISM IN TAROT:

Materiality and physicality: Earth represents the physical world, material possessions, and the body.

Stability and security: Earth is linked to stability, security, and a grounded approach to life.

Practicality: The element of Earth signifies practicality, hard work, and the importance of tangible results.

Growth and abundance: Earth represents growth, abundance, and the cycles of nature.

Themes: Material wealth, stability, and practical achievements

Example cards: Ace of Pentacles (new financial opportunity), Ten of Pentacles (wealth and family legacy), Queen of Pentacles (nurturing and resourcefulness)

Swords: Air

Element: Air
Associated qualities: Intellect, communication, truth, clarity, and conflict

AIR SYMBOLISM IN TAROT:

Intellect and thought: Air represents the mind, intellectual pursuits, and clarity of thought.

Communication: Air is associated with communication, both verbal and written, and the exchange of ideas.

Truth and clarity: The element of Air signifies truth, clarity, and the uncovering of hidden aspects.

Conflict and struggle: Air also represents conflict, struggle, and the challenges that lead to growth.

Themes: Ideas, conflict, truth, and mental clarity

Example cards: Ace of Swords (new ideas and clarity), Three of Swords (heartbreak and sorrow), King of Swords (authority and intellect)

Understanding the elements associated with each suit in the Tarot provides a foundational layer for interpreting the cards. Each element brings its unique qualities and influences, enriching the meanings of the cards and offering deeper insights into their messages. By recognizing these elemental associations, you can enhance your Tarot readings and connect more profoundly with the cards' energies and themes.

THE MAJOR ARCANA

0: The Fool

the FOOL.

CARD IMAGERY

The Fool card symbolizes new beginnings, unbridled optimism, and the courage to embark on a journey into the unknown. The imagery on this card highlights themes of innocence, spontaneity, and the willingness to take risks.

The jack-in-the-box: At the heart of the Fool card lies the joyful representation of a jack-in-the-box. This delightful figure embodies the essence of childlike wonder, reminding us of the unspoiled curiosity and untamed enthusiasm that often accompanies the beginning of a new journey. Like the figure popping out of the box, the Fool approaches life with a carefree attitude and a willingness to embrace the unexpected.

The dog on the latch: This loyal companion symbolizes the influence of those around us who may express concern or caution as we step into the unknown. While the Fool's journey is marked by exuberance, the presence of the dog highlights the importance of maintaining a balance between uninhibited enthusiasm and thoughtful consideration, acknowledging the value of external guidance.

The sun: The sun represents a divine source of guidance and inspiration that illuminates the Fool's path. As the sun provides light, clarity, and direction, it encourages the Fool to trust in a higher purpose and navigate the journey with optimism and assurance.

Water: Water symbolizes the subconscious realm and the emotional undercurrents that shape our decisions. The Fool's choice to step onto this watery path signifies a deliberate transition from introspection to action, from the inner world to the outer world. This movement reflects a bold willingness to embrace challenges and opportunities, guided by conscious and subconscious influences.

White flowers: These blossoms signify the Fool's untarnished spirit and the purity of intentions. Like the flowers, the Fool holds no preconceived notions or judgments, allowing for a genuine and unfiltered experience of life's wonders.

MEANING IN A TAROT READING

When the Fool card appears in a reading, it speaks to the themes of new beginnings, innocence, and the courage to embrace the unknown. It suggests that you are on the brink of a new adventure and encourages you to trust in the journey ahead.

New beginnings: The Fool card is associated with fresh starts, opportunities, and a willingness to enter the unknown. It signifies a clean slate and the potential for growth and change in various aspects of life.

Innocence and naivety: The Fool embodies a sense of childlike innocence and naivety. It represents approaching situations with an open heart, free from preconceived notions or biases. This can sometimes lead to unexpected outcomes, both positive and challenging.

Taking risks: The Fool encourages a willingness to take risks and embrace uncertainty. It suggests that sometimes, to achieve personal growth and fulfillment, one must venture into uncharted territory and overcome fears.

Trusting the journey: The Fool encourages trust in life's journey. It suggests that even though the path may not always be clear or easy, a sense of divine guidance or inner wisdom can lead the way.

Spontaneity and playfulness: The Fool represents a carefree and spontaneous attitude. It reminds us of the importance of enjoying the present moment, embracing spontaneity, and not taking life too seriously.

Letting go: The Fool encourages releasing attachments to the past and stepping into a future unburdened by past mistakes or regrets. It's a card of liberation and freedom from limitations.

Embracing change: The Fool card often appears when significant changes are on the horizon. It suggests being open to transformation and adapting to new circumstances with enthusiasm.

Inner wisdom: While the Fool may appear reckless on the surface, it also signifies a deeper connection to intuition and inner wisdom. The Fool trusts their inner guidance and listens to their heart.

It's important to note that the interpretation of the Fool card can vary depending on its placement in a Tarot spread and the surrounding cards. While the Fool embodies positive qualities, it can warn about impulsive decisions, overconfidence, or a lack of foresight.

THE FOOL (REVERSED)

When reversed, the Fool indicates a reckless or naive approach to a new journey. You might be embarking on a path without sufficient preparation or consideration of the consequences. This card warns against impulsive decisions and encourages you to ground yourself. There could be a sense of acting without thinking, leading to potential missteps. Reevaluate your plans and ensure you have a solid foundation before proceeding. Avoid taking unnecessary risks and seek advice from those with more experience.

1: The Magician

CARD IMAGERY

The Magician card traditionally symbolizes the power of transformation, mastery over elements, and the ability to manifest one's desires. In this deck, the Magician takes on a profound twist as it transforms into the Shaman—a symbol of spiritual connection, healing, and the seamless merging of earthly and cosmic energies. This reinterpretation brings a refreshing perspective to the card's symbolism, with the Shaman harnessing the energies of creation and manifestation for the well-being of both self and others.

Ouroboros: At the heart of the Shaman card lies the ouroboros, a symbol of eternal cycles and the interconnectedness of life, death, and rebirth. This emblem illustrates the Shaman's ability to navigate the infinite cosmic rhythms, reflecting his role in guiding individuals through personal transformation and growth.

Elements of the Tarot: The Shaman card prominently displays the four elemental symbols—Cups, Pentacles, Swords, and Wands. These elements signify the comprehensive mastery possessed by the Shaman. Representing emotions, material wealth, intellect, and inspiration, respectively, the Shaman has the tools to manifest intentions across all facets of existence.

Rose: The rose adorning the card represents love—an essential component of the Shaman's healing journey. Love serves as a driving force, motivating the Shaman to channel compassion, empathy, and positive energies into his healing endeavors.

Lilies: The serene lilies woven into the card's imagery symbolize true purpose. As the Shaman walks the path of healing, he embodies a profound sense of purpose and destiny, guiding others toward discovering their authentic paths.

River: The river embodies the Shaman's remarkable ability to manifest thoughts, ideas, and dreams into tangible reality. Just as a river shapes the landscape over time, the Shaman shapes his own reality and helps others do the same.

MEANING IN A TAROT READING

When the Magician card appears in a reading, it speaks to the themes of manifestation, skill, and the power to transform one's reality. It suggests that you have the tools and abilities to achieve your goals and encourages you to take decisive action.

Manifestation and action: The Magician signifies the power to turn your intentions into reality. It suggests that you have the tools, skills, and abilities to achieve your goals and dreams. This card encourages you to take initiative, make things happen, and act on your ideas.

Skill and mastery: The Magician represents mastery over various areas of life, often suggesting that you possess the knowledge and expertise needed to handle a situation. It can indicate a time of competence, where your abilities are being used well.

Transformation and change: Drawing the Magician can indicate a period of transformation and change. It suggests you can transform your circumstances, reshape your reality, and confidently embrace change.

Creative potential: This card is associated with creativity and innovative thinking. It suggests that you have a creative spark and the ability to develop novel solutions to challenges you may be facing.

Confidence and self-assertion: The Magician encourages you to believe in yourself and your abilities. It reminds you to have confidence in your decisions and actions. It also suggests the need to assert yourself and take control of a situation.

Alignment with higher purpose: The Magician is often seen as a bridge between the spiritual and physical realms. Drawing this card can indicate that you align with your higher purpose and that a deeper sense of meaning guides your actions.

Initiation and new beginnings: Just as the Fool card represents new beginnings, the Magician also signifies the start of a new phase or project. It's a card of initiation, suggesting that you embark on a journey with a strong sense of purpose and intention.

Use of resources: The Magician card emphasizes the importance of utilizing your resources wisely. It suggests that you have all the tools you need, and now is the time to make the most of them.

It's important to note that while the Magician card is generally positive and empowering, its interpretation can be influenced by the specific question and the other cards in the reading. It can also indicate the need for balance, ethical considerations, and awareness of any potential manipulation or misuse of power.

THE MAGICIAN (REVERSED)
In reverse, the Magician warns of deception, trickery, or misuse of power. You may not be utilizing your skills effectively, leading to feelings of inadequacy or frustration. There could be manipulation at play, either from others

or within yourself. This card urges you to examine your intentions and methods. Ensure that your actions align with your values and that you are using your talents for the right reasons. Avoid shortcuts and focus on ethical approaches to achieve your goals.

2: The High Priestess

CARD IMAGERY

The High Priestess card symbolizes intuition, esoteric knowledge, and the connection between the conscious and subconscious realms. The imagery on this card highlights themes of mystery, balance, and the hidden depths of the inner world.

Two pillars (B and J): Adorning the card are the pillars B and J, symbolizing Boaz and Jachin, the legendary pillars of King Solomon's temple. These pillars represent the dualistic nature of existence—the balance between opposites, such as light and darkness, masculine and feminine, and knowledge and mystery. The High Priestess, positioned between these pillars, embodies the harmonious equilibrium of these opposing forces, offering seekers a path of wisdom and balance.

The moon (waxing and waning): The waxing and waning moon adorning the High Priestess card represents the cycles of the subconscious mind. Just as the moon's phases influence the tides, the High Priestess taps into the ebb and flow of the subconscious, offering insights into hidden truths, intuitive guidance, and the mysteries beneath the surface.

Pomegranate: Symbolizes fertility and feminine energy and embodies the High Priestess's connection to the divine feminine. It signifies her role as a channel for intuitive and nurturing energies, inviting seekers to embrace their intuitive side and tap into the fertile depths of their inner wisdom.

Scroll: The scroll below the High Priestess represents spiritual knowledge and ancient wisdom. As the guardian of esoteric teachings, the High Priestess invites seekers to open the scroll of their consciousness and explore the depths of their spiritual understanding. She serves as a guide to uncovering hidden truths and embracing inner illumination.

Stained-glass window: The stained-glass window is a symbolic barrier between the earthly realm and the realm beyond. It represents the veil that separates the mundane from the mystical, the tangible from the intangible. Through this window, the High Priestess gazes beyond the veil, connecting with higher realms of consciousness and bringing forth insights and revelations from the divine.

MEANING IN A TAROT READING

When the High Priestess card appears in a reading, it speaks to the themes of intuition, hidden knowledge, and exploring the subconscious mind. It suggests a time to trust your inner wisdom and delve into the mysteries that lie beneath the surface.

Intuition and inner knowing: The High Priestess highlights the importance of listening to your intuition and trusting your gut feelings. It encourages you to pay attention to the subtle messages from your subconscious mind.

Mystery and hidden truths: This card signifies the presence of hidden truths and the need to explore the deeper aspects of your psyche. It invites you to uncover the mysteries that lie beyond the everyday world and to embrace the unknown.

Balance and equilibrium: The High Priestess embodies the balance between opposites, such as light and darkness, masculine and feminine. This card encourages you to find harmony and equilibrium in your life, integrating different aspects of your being.

Spiritual knowledge: The scroll represents the esoteric knowledge and ancient wisdom that the High Priestess guards. This card invites you to seek spiritual insights and to explore the depths of your spiritual understanding.

Divine feminine: The pomegranate symbolizes the connection to the divine feminine and the nurturing, intuitive energies that the High Priestess channels. This card encourages you to embrace your inner femininity and tap into the fertile depths of your inner wisdom.

Revelations and insights: The stained-glass window represents the veil between the mundane and the mystical. The High Priestess allows you to pierce this veil and receive insights and revelations from higher realms of consciousness.

The High Priestess card is a profound reminder of the importance of intuition, hidden knowledge, and the exploration of the subconscious mind. It invites you to trust your inner wisdom, embrace the mysteries that lie beyond the surface, and seek balance and harmony in your life. This card encourages you to delve into the depths of your psyche, uncover hidden truths, and embrace the divine guidance that comes from within. Listen to your inner voice, follow your heart's nudges, and embark on a journey of self-discovery and spiritual growth.

THE HIGH PRIESTESS (REVERSED)
Reversed, the High Priestess suggests secrets, hidden agendas, or a disconnect from your intuition. You may be ignoring your inner voice, leading to confusion or misguided decisions. This card highlights the need for introspection and self-awareness. There could be hidden information or deceit affecting your situation. Trust your instincts and take time to uncover the truth. Meditative practices can help reconnect you with your inner wisdom and provide clarity.

3: The Empress

CARD IMAGERY
The Empress card embodies the divine feminine energy in its fullest expression. She epitomizes fertility, abundance, and creativity, seated on a lush, verdant throne nestled within a fertile landscape. Her presence radiates warmth and nurturing energy, inviting all who approach her to experience the richness and abundance of the natural world.

The crown: Adorned with twelve shimmering stars, it symbolizes unity and harmony. Each star represents a unique aspect of the cosmic forces, emphasizing the interconnectedness of all living beings with the celestial realms.

Three-tiered crown: The crown is a testament to the multifaceted nature of femininity. The tiers represent the stages of a woman's life journey: the maiden (youthful vitality and potential), the mother (nurturing and fertility), and the crone (wisdom and maturity). As the embodiment of the divine feminine, the Empress encompasses the entire spectrum of womanhood.

Cornucopia: In one of her hands, the Empress cradles a cornucopia overflowing with ripe fruits, grains, and flowers. The horn of plenty symbolizes the inexhaustible flow of creative energy and abundance emanating from her being. It emphasizes the Empress's role as a source of life and sustenance, embodying fertility, prosperity, and the nurturing power of Mother Earth.

Fields of golden wheat: Fields of golden wheat sway in the gentle breeze, ready for harvesting. The wheat represents the fruition of her creative endeavors and the abundance that arises from nurturing and cultivating life. It serves as a reminder of the cycles of nature and the cyclical nature of life, where growth and renewal are perpetual.

Scepter: In the bottom border there is a scepter adorned with intricate carvings and symbols of authority. This scepter symbolizes her sovereignty and power as the ruler of her own domain. With confidence and grace, she governs with wisdom and compassion, ensuring harmony and abundance for all who dwell within her realm. This image of authority and power can inspire you to embrace your sovereignty and govern your life with wisdom and compassion.

MEANING IN A TAROT READING

When the Empress card appears in a reading, it speaks to the themes of growth, abundance, and creativity in their purest forms. It suggests a time of expansion, nurturing, and the fruition of your endeavors.

Growth and abundance: The Empress represents a period of growth, abundance, and creativity. She encourages you to embrace the nurturing energy within yourself, which can help you cultivate abundance and creativity in all aspects of your life.

Nurturing and fertility: As a symbol of fertility and prosperity, the Empress encourages you to connect with the natural world, nurture yourself and others, and trust in the universe's abundance.

Creative potential: This card signifies a time of expansion and fruition, where new opportunities and creative ventures abound. It encourages you to embrace your creative potential, nurture your dreams and aspirations, and trust in the abundance of the universe.

Cycles of nature: The Empress reminds you to honor the cycles of nature, cultivate harmony and balance in your life, and embrace the power of creation and manifestation.

Sovereignty and authority: The scepter symbolizes sovereignty and the power to govern your own life with wisdom and compassion. This card inspires you to embrace your own sovereignty and govern your life with confidence and grace.

The Empress card reminds us of the importance of nurturing energy, growth, and creativity in our lives. It invites us to connect with the natural world, trust in the abundance of the universe, and embrace the cycles of nature. This card encourages us to nurture our dreams and aspirations, embrace our creative potential, and govern our lives with wisdom and compassion.

THE EMPRESS (REVERSED)

When the Empress is reversed, it can signify issues with fertility, creativity, or nurturing. You might be feeling blocked or disconnected from your natural flow of abundance and care. There may be difficulties in expressing your creativity or taking care of yourself and others. This card encourages you to reevaluate your self-care routines and reconnect with your creative energy. Focus on nurturing yourself and addressing any emotional or physical imbalances.

4: The Emperor

CARD IMAGERY

The Emperor card stands tall and regal, embodying authority, structure, and control. Seated upon a magnificent throne, he commands attention and respect, his presence radiating power and wisdom. Adorned with symbols of sovereignty, the Emperor represents the pinnacle of leadership and governance.

Rams' heads: Flanking the Emperor's throne are the heads of rams, representing Khnum, the Egyptian aspect of Ra, the god of creation. This symbolizes the Emperor's divine connection to the creative forces of the universe, highlighting his ability to shape and mold his reality according to his will.

Constellation of Aries: Above the Emperor's head, the constellation of Aries shines brightly, signifying courage, initiative, and assertiveness. It underscores the

Emperor's capacity to take bold action, lead with confidence, and pioneer new paths.

Crown: This card depicts a majestic crown, symbolizing autonomy, self-direction, and authority. It signifies his sovereign rule over his domain and his ability to make wise and purposeful decisions that shape the course of events.

Ankh: Below the Emperor is the ankh, an ancient Egyptian symbol of life and vitality. It represents masculine virility, strength, and vitality, underscoring the Emperor's ability to harness his energy and drive to achieve his goals.

Armor: The Emperor is clad in sturdy armor, symbolizing protection, resilience, and strength. It reflects his ability to defend himself and others, as well as to overcome obstacles and challenges with unwavering determination.

Wintry landscape: Surrounding the Emperor is a wintry landscape, evoking the duality of night and day. This symbolizes the Emperor's mastery over all aspects of himself, including both light and shadow. It highlights his inner strength and stability, even in the face of adversity.

Throne: The Emperor sits upon a grand throne, symbolizing power, authority, and might. It represents his position of leadership and governance and his responsibility to establish order and structure in his realm.

MEANING IN A TAROT READING

When the Emperor card appears in a reading, it speaks to the themes of authority, structure, and leadership. It suggests that you are in a position of power and influence and encourages you to take charge of your life.

Authority and leadership: The Emperor symbolizes authority and leadership, suggesting that you are in a position of power and influence. It encourages you to assert your authority with confidence and integrity.

Structure and discipline: The Emperor reminds you of the importance of structure and discipline in achieving your goals. It advises you to establish clear boundaries, set realistic goals, and follow through with determination and perseverance.

Stability and security: The Emperor represents stability and security, indicating that you have the strength and resilience to overcome challenges and succeed. It encourages you to trust in your abilities and take decisive action to create a solid foundation for the future.

Strategic planning: The Emperor encourages you to take a strategic approach to your endeavors, carefully considering your options and making well-informed decisions. It advises you to think ahead, anticipate obstacles, and plan for the long term.

Personal authority: On a deeper level, the Emperor urges you to embrace your authority and stand in your power. It reminds you to honor your values, assert your boundaries, and take ownership of your life and choices.

The Emperor card serves as a powerful reminder of the importance of leadership, structure, and resilience. It invites you to embody these qualities as you navigate through life's challenges, to trust in your inner wisdom, and to assert your authority with confidence. This card encourages you to manifest your desires and achieve your goals by taking a strategic, disciplined approach and maintaining stability and security in your life.

THE EMPEROR (REVERSED)

Reversed, the Emperor points to a misuse of authority, rigidity, or lack of control. You may be facing issues with power dynamics, either by exerting too much control or being controlled by others. This card suggests that you reassess your leadership style and approach situations with flexibility. There could be a need to establish boundaries or address issues of dominance. Strive for balance and fairness in your dealings and embrace a more collaborative approach.

5: The Hierophant

CARD IMAGERY

The Hierophant card in this deck is a profound symbol of spiritual authority, wisdom, and tradition. The imagery on this card is rich with symbols that convey its deeper meanings and significance.

Papal crown: The papal crown sits atop the Hierophant's head, a powerful symbol of authority and connection to the divine. This crown signifies a person in a position of leadership and represents the Holy Trinity, emphasizing the unity and sanctity of the divine presence.

Blessing hand: To the left of the Hierophant is a hand posing in a specific gesture of blessing. Above the fingers are the Greek initials for Jesus Christ (I C X C), further reinforcing the card's connection to spiritual guidance and divine blessing. This hand symbolizes the transmission of sacred wisdom and the act of bestowing blessings upon those who seek it.

All-seeing eye: To the right of the Hierophant, the all-seeing eye symbolizes truth and knowledge gained through experience. It represents the understanding from a higher perspective, offering insight and clarity to those who are open to its vision.

Hands of worship: The borders depict two hands of worship below the Hierophant. These hands signify reverence and respect, highlighting the Hierophant's role as a revered leader and a respected figure in spiritual matters.

Statue form: The Hierophant is depicted as a statue, emphasizing solidity, permanence, and authority. This statue form contrasts with the stained-glass window of the High Priestess card, indicating a grounded, authoritative presence in contrast to the ethereal, intuitive nature of the High Priestess.

Three circles: Behind the Hierophant statue are three circles again referencing the Holy Trinity. These circles underscore the divine connection and the cyclical nature of spiritual wisdom and teachings.

MEANING IN A TAROT READING

When the Hierophant card appears in a reading, it signifies a call to embrace tradition, seek spiritual guidance, and adhere to established moral codes and values. This card often represents institutions, religious or otherwise, and can indicate a need for conventional wisdom and conformity to established norms.

Authority and leadership: The Hierophant embodies the role of a spiritual or authoritative leader who can offer guidance and wisdom based on experience and knowledge. This card may suggest seeking counsel from a mentor or a respected figure in your life.

Spiritual guidance: The symbols of the papal crown and the blessing hand point to the importance of spiritual teachings and the blessings that come from following a path of faith and devotion. This card encourages you to seek deeper understanding through traditional practices and rituals.

Truth and knowledge: The all-seeing eye reminds us that true wisdom comes from experience and a higher perspective. It invites us to look beyond the surface and seek the underlying truth in our situations.

Respect and reverence: The hands of worship emphasize the importance of respect for tradition and reverence for the spiritual journey. This card calls for a humble approach to learning and a respectful acknowledgment of the wisdom passed down through generations.

Solid foundations: The Hierophant's statue form suggests the importance of solid foundations and a stable structure in your spiritual or personal life. It encourages you to build upon established principles and values to create a lasting and meaningful legacy.

The Hierophant card serves as a reminder of the power of tradition, the value of spiritual guidance, and the importance of truth and reverence in our lives. It encourages us to seek wisdom from established sources and to honor the teachings that have shaped our understanding of the world.

THE HIEROPHANT (REVERSED)
In reverse, the Hierophant suggests nonconformity, rebellion, or challenges to traditional beliefs. You may be questioning established norms or feeling restricted by societal expectations. This card encourages you to embrace your individuality and explore alternative paths.

There could be a desire to break free from conventional structures and seek your own truth. Be open to new ideas and perspectives but also consider the wisdom that tradition can offer.

6: The Lovers

CARD IMAGERY
The Lovers card in this deck is a rich tapestry of symbols that delve into love, choice, duality, and destiny themes. Each element on this card adds depth to its meaning, offering a nuanced perspective on relationships and personal decisions.

Star-crossed lovers: Within the silhouette of the two lovers, stars shine brightly, symbolizing destiny or fate. This imagery suggests that these individuals' connections are written in the stars, indicating a powerful, almost fated bond.

Apple tree: The apple tree, a direct reference to the Garden of Eden, symbolizes temptation and the pivotal choices that define one's path. It recalls the story of Eve and the serpent, highlighting themes of knowledge, temptation, and the consequences of our decisions.

Constellation of Gemini: The stars form the constellation of Gemini, emphasizing the astrological significance of the card. Gemini, associated with duality and choice, underscores the importance of balance and the interplay of opposites in relationships.

Serpent: The serpent coiled around the apple tree reinforces the theme of temptation. It reminds us of the challenges and moral dilemmas that often accompany decisions related to love and desire.

Angel wings: At the top of the card, the wings of archangel Raphael spread wide, symbolizing divine love and healing. Raphael, the angel of love, guides and blesses the lovers, suggesting that their union is under the protection and guidance of higher powers.

Inner flame: The flame at the bottom border represents the inner flame of passion and the heart's urging. It signifies the importance of making choices based on true desires and emotional truths rather than purely rational considerations.

MEANING IN A TAROT READING

When the Lovers card appears in a reading, it speaks to themes of love, connection, and choice. It often signifies important relationships, be they romantic, platonic, or familial, and the decisions that impact these bonds.

Love and connection: The Lovers card is a powerful indicator of deep emotional bonds and meaningful relationships. It may point to a significant romantic relationship or a deep connection with another person that profoundly influences your life.

Choice and duality: With the constellation of Gemini and the symbolism of the apple tree and serpent, this card emphasizes the importance of choices. It reminds you that every relationship and situation come with decisions that have significant consequences, urging careful consideration.

Temptation and consequence: The serpent and the apple tree harken back to the story of temptation in the Garden of Eden, suggesting that you may be faced with moral dilemmas or enticing offers that require thoughtful deliberation.

Divine guidance and healing: Archangel Raphael's angel wings indicate that your relationships and choices are under the watchful eye of divine guidance. Raphael's presence suggests healing, support, and blessings, encouraging you to trust the higher powers overseeing your journey.

Inner passion: The flame at the card's bottom border symbolizes the inner fire that drives your decisions. It encourages you to listen to your heart and make choices that align with your passions and desires.

The Lovers card in this deck is a profound symbol of the complexities of love, the importance of choices, and the interplay between destiny and free will. It invites you to consider the deeper connections in your life, the moral and emotional decisions you face, and the divine guidance that supports your journey.

THE LOVERS (REVERSED)
When reversed, the Lovers can indicate disharmony, imbalance, or difficult choices in relationships. You may be experiencing conflicts, misalignments, or doubts about your partnerships. This card highlights the importance of making choices that honor your true self. Reflect on your values and ensure that your relationships align with your authentic desires. Open communication and honest self-assessment are crucial to resolving conflicts and finding harmony.

7: The Chariot

CARD IMAGERY

The Chariot card symbolizes determination, direction, and the drive to achieve one's goals. The rich symbolism on this card provides a multifaceted perspective on movement, control, and the journey ahead.

Two sphinxes: The black and white sphinxes, each embodying elements of human, eagle, lion, and bull, represent unity in diversity. They symbolize the four elements—Air, Wind, Fire, and Earth—indicating a balance of forces and the importance of harmonizing different aspects of life to move forward successfully.

Magic wand: Positioned at the bottom of the card, the magic wand draws reference to the Magician. This wand signifies creativity and initiative, suggesting that the charioteer possesses the skills and determination of the Magician, now applied in motion and action.

Comet: Unique to this deck, the comet symbolizes direction, fire, and focus. It represents a guiding force, illuminating the path ahead and highlighting the importance of staying on course with intensity and purpose.

Canopy of stars: Above the charioteer is a canopy of stars, symbolizing hope and vision. This element underscores the importance of having a clear vision and aspirations, guiding the journey with a sense of purpose and celestial support.

Wheels of the Chariot: The wheels symbolize movement and the rapid achievement of goals. They signify progress and the momentum needed to reach one's objectives efficiently and effectively.

City outline against the night sky: The city silhouette against the dark sky represents leaving the safety and familiarity of home to embark on a quest. It highlights the courage to venture into the unknown and the promise of new adventures and discoveries.

MEANING IN A TAROT READING

When the Chariot card appears in a reading, it is a powerful indicator of determination, control, and the drive to overcome obstacles and achieve success. It speaks to the energy of movement and the focus required to reach one's goals.

Determination and willpower: The Chariot signifies strong willpower and determination. It suggests that you have the inner strength and resolve to overcome any challenges in your path and to push forward toward your goals with confidence and focus.

Balancing forces: The black and white sphinxes highlight the need to balance opposing forces. This card encourages you to harmonize different aspects of your life, integrating diverse elements to create a unified direction and purpose.

Creativity and initiative: The magic wand at the bottom of the card reminds you to harness your creativity and initiative. Like the Magician, you have the tools and skills to shape your destiny and actively pursue your objectives.

Focus and direction: The comet reminds us of the importance of maintaining focus and direction. It encourages us to stay on course, driven by a fiery passion and a clear sense of purpose, knowing that our path is illuminated.

Hope and vision: The canopy of stars provides a sense of hope and vision. This element suggests that a higher purpose guides your journey, and that the universe supports your aspirations.

Movement and progress: The chariot's wheels emphasize rapid movement and progress. This card signals that you are in a phase of active pursuit, where momentum is on your side and goals can be achieved swiftly.

Venturing beyond comfort: The city outline against the night sky indicates the courage to leave your comfort zone. True growth and success often come from stepping into the unknown and embracing new challenges and adventures.

The Chariot card symbolizes the dynamic energy of progress, the balance of diverse forces, and the drive to achieve your goals with determination and vision. It invites you to harness your inner strength, stay focused on your path, and embrace the journey ahead confidently and clearly.

THE CHARIOT (REVERSED)

Reversed, the Chariot signifies lack of direction, control issues, and potential obstacles. You might be feeling stuck or overwhelmed by challenges, leading to frustration and loss of motivation. This card urges you to regain control and set clear, achievable goals. There could be internal or external conflicts hindering your progress. Focus on aligning your efforts and maintaining determination. Seek balance between ambition and patience to move forward effectively. Be cautious of pushing too hard or being too passive—find the middle ground where you can steer your course with confidence. Reevaluate your path, adjust strategies, and harness your willpower to overcome setbacks.

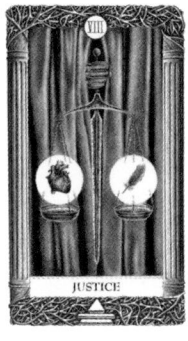

8: Justice

CARD IMAGERY
The Justice card embodies the principles of fairness, balance, and impartiality. Its intricate symbolism provides a deep understanding of justice, truth, and the consequences of our actions.

Curtains: The curtains behind the figure of Justice symbolize the concept of impartial justice. They indicate that true justice is impartial and unbiased, free from external influences or personal prejudices.

Fulcrum of the scales: The sword, acting as the fulcrum of the scales, emphasizes that action results from judgment. The sword represents the power and decisiveness necessary to implement justice, while the scales signify the careful weighing of options and evidence.

Heart and feather: The heart and feather on opposite scale plates refer to the ancient Egyptian belief that Anubis weighed the heart against a feather to judge the virtue of one's life. This symbolizes the moral and ethical balance in determining justice, weighing one's actions and intentions.

Stone pillars: The stone pillars flanking the figure represent the permanence and rigidity of law. They signify the unchanging and steadfast nature of true justice, grounded in fundamental principles and structures.

Alchemy symbol for Air: The alchemy symbol for air at the bottom border denotes that the Justice card is aligned with the Air element, representing the mind and intellect. The symbol highlights the importance of rational thought, clarity, and logic in pursuing justice.

Scales: The scales directly represent fairness and truth. They emphasize the necessity of balanced judgment and the pursuit of equity in all matters.

MEANING IN A TAROT READING

When the Justice card appears in a reading, it calls attention to themes of fairness, balance, and ethical integrity. It suggests that you are in a position where careful consideration and impartial judgment are required.

Fairness and Impartiality: Justice signifies the need for fairness and impartiality. It encourages you to approach situations with an open mind, free from biases, ensuring that your decisions are just and equitable.

Consequences of actions: The sword and scales together remind you that your actions have consequences. This card urges you to consider the potential outcomes of your decisions and to act with integrity and responsibility.

Moral and ethical balance: The heart and feather symbolism highlights the importance of balancing moral and ethical considerations. Justice asks you to weigh your heart's intentions against the truth, ensuring that your actions align with your values.

Rational thought: With the Air element representing the mind and intellect, this card emphasizes the need for clear, rational thinking. It encourages you to use logic and reason when making decisions, cutting through confusion and ambiguity.

Structure and law: The stone pillars signify the importance of adhering to established laws and principles. Justice calls for respect for legal and ethical frameworks, reminding you that these structures provide stability and fairness in society.

Truth and integrity: The scales of justice underscore the pursuit of truth and integrity. This card urges you to seek the truth in all situations and act honestly and transparently.

The Justice card serves as a powerful reminder of the importance of fairness, balance, and ethical integrity. It invites you to approach situations with a clear mind, to weigh your actions carefully, and to act in alignment with your highest values and principles.

JUSTICE (REVERSED)

Reversed, Justice points to imbalance, unfairness, and dishonesty. You may be dealing with legal issues, facing injustice, or feeling wronged in some way. This card highlights the need to strive for fairness and seek the truth in all matters. There could be a need to address ethical dilemmas and restore balance in your life. Focus on honesty, accountability, and making decisions that align with your moral values.

9: The Hermit

CARD IMAGERY

The Hermit card embodies the quest for inner wisdom, introspection, and guidance from within. Each symbol on this card contributes to the profound message of self-reflection and spiritual enlightenment.

The old man: Depicted as the archetype of wisdom, the old man with his beard, hood, and direct gaze represents the sage who seeks truth and knowledge. His presence on the card emphasizes the importance of wisdom gained through life experiences and deep contemplation.

Staff in the border: The staff symbolizes self-support and the journey inward. It represents the strength and stability that come from relying on oneself and turning inward for answers and guidance.

The lantern: The lantern held by the Hermit signifies the inner divine light that illuminates the way. It is a beacon of hope and clarity, guiding you through the darkness of uncertainty and leading you toward self-awareness and understanding.

The six-pointed star: Within the lantern, the six-pointed star is a symbol of hope and guidance. It reminds you that even in solitude and introspection, there is a guiding light that offers direction and reassurance.

Hourglass on its side: The hourglass lying on its side indicates the necessity of taking time for self-examination. It suggests that there is no need to rush this process; instead, you should allow yourself the time to reflect and explore your inner world thoroughly. This symbol emphasizes the importance of pausing and stopping the clock to focus on your internal journey before moving forward.

MEANING IN A TAROT READING

When the Hermit card appears in a reading, it calls for introspection, solitude, and the pursuit of inner wisdom. It signifies a period when looking inward and seeking personal truth is essential for growth and understanding.

Introspection and solitude: The Hermit encourages you to seek solitude and quiet reflection. This card suggests that now is the time to withdraw from external distractions and focus on your inner world, exploring your thoughts, feelings, and spiritual path.

Inner wisdom: The old man symbolizes the wisdom that comes from within. The Hermit card indicates that you possess the knowledge and insight needed to navigate your current situation, and it encourages you to trust your inner guidance.

Self-support and strength: The staff in the border represents the support and strength you can find within yourself. This card reminds you that you have the resources and resilience to support yourself through periods of introspection and self-discovery.

Illumination and clarity: The lantern signifies the inner light that illuminates your path. The Hermit suggests that by turning inward and seeking your own truth, you will gain clarity and insight that will guide you forward.

Hope and guidance: The six-pointed star offers a message of hope and guidance. Even in times of solitude and introspection, this card reassures you that there is a guiding light leading you toward understanding and enlightenment.

Taking time for self-examination: The hourglass on the side emphasizes the importance of taking your time with the process of self-examination. The Hermit advises you not to rush but to allow yourself the necessary time to reflect and gain a deeper understanding of yourself and your path.

Overall, the Hermit serves as a profound symbol of the importance of introspection, inner wisdom, and the guidance that comes from within. It invites you to embrace solitude, trust your inner light, and take the time needed to explore your inner landscape before proceeding on your journey.

THE HERMIT (REVERSED)
Reversed, the Hermit suggests isolation, loneliness, and avoidance of necessary introspection. You might be withdrawing from others or avoiding self-reflection, leading to feelings of disconnection. This card encourages you to balance solitude with social interactions. There could be a need to seek inner guidance and confront your inner fears. Use this time to reconnect with your spiritual self and gain deeper understanding of your path.

10: The Wheel of Fortune

CARD IMAGERY
The Wheel of Fortune card captures the essence of life's cycles, the influence of fate, and the interconnectedness of all things. Its rich symbolism provides a profound understanding of the ebb and flow of life and the eternal nature of change.

The four elements: These symbols represent Water, Air, Earth, and Fire, highlighting the cyclical nature of the natural world. They remind us of the constant state of flux in life and the ongoing cycles of creation, transformation, and renewal.

Ouroboros: The ouroboros, a serpent eating its own tail, symbolizes infinity and the eternal cycle of life. It signifies the concept of something constantly re-creating itself, emphasizing the idea of perpetual change and the continuity of existence.

The angel, eagle, bull, and lion: These creatures represent the four evangelists—Matthew, Mark, Luke, and John—who spread the word of Christ to the four corners of the world. They symbolize the dissemination of knowledge, spiritual guidance, and the universal impact of divine messages.

The wheel: The central wheel represents the sun, a symbol of life, vitality, and the cyclical passage of time. It underscores the idea of the ever-turning wheel of fortune that governs the ups and downs of existence.

MEANING IN A TAROT READING

When the Wheel of Fortune card appears in a reading, it speaks to the forces of fate and change and the cyclical nature of life. It signifies a turning point and the inevitable positive or negative change.

Cycles and change: The Wheel of Fortune emphasizes the cyclical nature of life. It reminds you that change is a constant and that you are part of an ongoing cycle of beginnings and endings, growth and decay.

Fate and destiny: This card highlights the role of fate and destiny in your life. It suggests that events may be beyond your control, and it encourages you to embrace the unknown with an open heart, trusting that each turn of the wheel brings valuable lessons.

Interconnectedness: The presence of the four elements underscores the interconnectedness of all things. The Wheel of Fortune card invites you to recognize the links between various aspects of your life and to appreciate how each part contributes to the whole.

Spiritual guidance: The angel, eagle, bull, and lion represent spiritual guidance and the dissemination of wisdom. This card encourages you to seek and spread knowledge, understanding that divine messages and teachings can help navigate the cycles of life.

Eternal nature: The ouroboros symbolizes infinity and the eternal nature of cycles. The Wheel of Fortune reminds you that every ending is a new beginning and that life is a continuous transformation journey.

Vitality and renewal: The wheel as the sun signifies life force, vitality, and renewal. It encourages you to harness the energy of the present moment and to find strength in the knowledge that every phase, whether joyous or challenging, is part of the broader spectrum of life.

Overall, the Wheel of Fortune card serves as a profound symbol of the ever-changing nature of life, the influence of fate, and the interconnected cycles that shape our existence. It invites you to embrace change, trust in the journey, and recognize the wisdom and growth that come with each turn of the wheel.

THE WHEEL OF FORTUNE (REVERSED)
When the Wheel of Fortune is reversed, it indicates delays, setbacks, and resistance to change. You may be feeling stuck in a cycle of misfortune or unable to break free from challenging patterns. This card suggests that you embrace the lessons of the moment and be patient for the tides to turn. There could be a need to release control and trust in the natural flow of events. Focus on adaptability and resilience to navigate through difficult times.

11: Strength

CARD IMAGERY
The Strength card symbolizes the harmonious balance between inner power and gentleness, highlighting the strength found within patience and compassion. Its imagery emphasizes courage, resilience, and the beauty of inner strength.

Infinity symbol: Represents balance, renewal, consistency, and patience. It signifies the eternal cycle of growth and the enduring nature of true strength, cultivated over time and through continual effort.

Lion: The lion is a universal symbol of strength, power, courage, and majesty. It embodies the raw, untamed energy that lies within each of us, representing our capacity for bravery and resilience in the face of challenges.

The young woman: The young woman symbolizes innocence and gentle strength. Despite her appearance of vulnerability, she possesses an immense inner capacity to harness her strength and power, which the lion embodies. This imagery suggests that true strength often comes from within and is expressed through calmness and confidence.

Roses: Roses symbolize beauty, celebration, and protection. They highlight the idea that strength is not only about power but also about appreciating the beauty of life and celebrating achievements while maintaining a sense of protection and care.

MEANING IN A TAROT READING

When the Strength card appears in a reading, it speaks to the power of inner strength, patience, and the gentle yet resilient nature of true courage. It suggests that you have the inner resources needed to face challenges with grace and determination.

Inner strength and courage: The Strength card highlights your inner strength and courage. It encourages you to trust in your ability to overcome obstacles and face difficulties with a calm and confident demeanor.

Balance and patience: The infinity symbol reminds you of the importance of balance and patience. True strength comes from a consistent and balanced approach to life, allowing for renewal and growth.

Gentle power: The young woman and the lion together symbolize gentle power. This card teaches that strength is not always about force but can be found in gentleness, compassion, and the ability to remain calm and composed in the face of adversity.

Beauty and celebration: Roses signify beauty and celebration, reminding you to appreciate the beauty in your life and celebrate your accomplishments. They also represent the protective aspects of strength, suggesting that part of strength is knowing how to safeguard what you value.

Resilience and majesty: The lion's presence underscores the qualities of resilience and majesty. This card encourages you to embrace your power and to recognize the noble and courageous spirit within you.

Overall, the Strength card serves as a profound reminder of the power of inner strength, the importance of balance and patience, and the beauty of gentle resilience. It invites you to embrace your inner power, approach challenges with calm confidence, and celebrate the strength that lies within you.

STRENGTH (REVERSED)

In reverse, Strength points to self-doubt, fear, and misuse of power. You may be struggling with inner turmoil, feeling insecure, or lacking confidence in your abilities. This card suggests that you cultivate patience and inner resilience to overcome these challenges. There could be a need to address feelings of inadequacy and develop self-compassion. Embrace your strengths and acknowledge your vulnerabilities to build genuine inner courage.

12: The Hanged Man

CARD IMAGERY
The Hanged Man card symbolizes surrender, introspection, and a shift in perspective. The imagery highlights the importance of acceptance, patience, and the enlightenment that comes from seeing things from a different viewpoint.

The man: Upside down and restrained, he cannot free himself, but he is not struggling. This lack of struggle symbolizes the act of surrender and the willingness to accept one's circumstances without resistance.

The Halo: The halo represents his acceptance of his fate, indicating spiritual enlightenment and a higher understanding of his situation. It also symbolizes martyrdom, signifying the willingness to sacrifice and endure for the greater good.

The black background: Although it may seem that he is in a dark place, the light surrounding him indicates that he must be there. This suggests that there is a purpose even in moments of darkness, and the light will return.

MEANING IN A TAROT READING
When the Hanged Man card appears in a reading, it speaks to the need for surrender, patience, and a new perspective. You may need to let go of control and embrace the present moment to gain deeper insights and understanding.

Surrender and acceptance: The Hanged Man highlights the importance of surrendering to your current circumstances and accepting what is. It encourages you to let go of resistance and trust in the process of life.

New perspective: This card suggests that seeing things from a different viewpoint can bring enlightenment and clarity. Embrace the opportunity to look at situations from a new angle, which can lead to deeper understanding and growth.

Patience and stillness: The Hanged Man teaches the value of patience and stillness. It reminds you that sometimes the best action is inaction, allowing you to gain wisdom and insight through contemplation and reflection.

Spiritual enlightenment: The halo signifies spiritual awakening and the acceptance of one's fate. It encourages trust in the divine plan and recognition that there is a higher purpose behind one's experiences.

Navigating darkness: The black background suggests that even in dark times, your experiences have a reason. Trust that the light will return and that the period of introspection is necessary for your growth and transformation.

Overall, the Hanged Man card serves as a powerful reminder of the importance of surrender, patience, and a shift in perspective. It invites you to embrace stillness, trust in the divine timing, and seek enlightenment by viewing your circumstances from a new angle. This card encourages you to find peace in acceptance and to understand that even in darkness, there is a purpose, and the light will eventually return.

THE HANGED MAN (REVERSED)

In reverse, the Hanged Man suggests stubbornness, resistance to change, and feeling trapped. You might be avoiding necessary sacrifices or not seeing things from a different perspective. This card encourages you to let go and trust the process. There could be a need to release old patterns and embrace new ways of thinking. Practice patience and openness to gain deeper insights and clarity.

13: Death

CARD IMAGERY
The Death card symbolizes profound transformation, endings, and new beginnings. The card's imagery highlights the inevitability of change and the continuous cycle of life, death, and rebirth.

Two-headed phoenix in the shape of the infinity symbol: The phoenix symbolizes that death is not an ending but an opportunity for transformation and the beginning of a new cycle in life. The phoenix rising from its ashes represents renewal and the eternal nature of life.

The moth and the flame: The moth's attraction to the flame references the inevitability of death. This imagery suggests that change is an inescapable part of life, like the moth's attraction to the flame.

The hourglasses: The hourglasses indicate that time is running out, reminding us of the finite nature of our current experiences and the urgency to embrace change and transformation.

MEANING IN A TAROT READING
When the Death card appears in a reading, it speaks to the themes of transformation, endings, and new beginnings. It suggests that you are undergoing a significant

period of change that will lead to profound personal growth and renewal.

Transformation and renewal: The Death card highlights embracing change as a natural part of life. It encourages you to let go of the old and welcome the new, understanding that transformation is essential for growth.

Endings and beginnings: This card signifies that one phase of your life is ending, making way for a new beginning. It reminds you that endings are necessary to create space for new opportunities and experiences.

Inevitability of change: The moth and the flame emphasize that change is an inevitable part of life. Rather than resisting it, embrace the transformative power of change and trust in the process.

Urgency and time: The hourglasses remind us that time is running out. Use this awareness to motivate yourself to embrace change and make the most of the present moment, knowing that life is continually evolving.

Eternal cycle: The two-headed phoenix in the shape of the infinity symbol underscores the eternal cycle of life, death, and rebirth. It reassures you that every ending leads to a new beginning, and every transformation brings renewal and growth.

Overall, the Death card is a powerful reminder of the inevitability of change and the transformative power of endings and new beginnings. It invites you to embrace the cycles of life, trust in the process of transformation, and understand that with every ending comes the opportunity for renewal and growth. This card encourages you to let go of what no longer serves you, and to welcome the new possibilities that lie ahead.

DEATH (REVERSED)

Reversed, Death indicates resistance to change, stagnation, and fear of transformation. You may be clinging to the past or afraid of letting go, leading to a sense of being stuck. This card suggests that you embrace the inevitable changes and allow for new beginnings. There could be a need to release old attachments and welcome transformation. Focus on the opportunities for growth that change brings.

14: Temperance

CARD IMAGERY

The Temperance card symbolizes balance, harmony, and the alchemy of transformation through patience and moderation. The imagery on this card highlights the spiritual and transformational process that comes from allowing gradual growth and evolution.

The cups: The cups represent the alchemy of turning water to gold. This symbolizes the transformative power of patience and the ability to blend different elements harmoniously to create something precious and new.

The sun rays: Signify the spiritual and transformational process. They remind us of the importance of patience and the slow, steady growth that comes from allowing natural evolution and alchemy.

Irises: The iris is a flower named after the Greek goddess Iris, symbolizing rainbows and hope. These flowers represent the beauty and promise of balance, harmony, and the blending of diverse elements.

MEANING IN A TAROT READING

When the Temperance card appears in a reading, it speaks to the themes of balance, moderation, and the alchemical transformation process. It suggests that you are blending different aspects of your life harmoniously and finding a sense of equilibrium.

Balance and harmony: The Temperance card highlights the importance of maintaining balance and harmony. It encourages you to blend different elements and find a middle path that integrates various aspects of your experiences.

Patience and moderation: This card suggests that patience and moderation are key to achieving your goals. Trust in gradual growth and transformation, knowing that slow and steady progress leads to lasting results.

Transformation and alchemy: The imagery of turning water to gold signifies the transformative power of patience and the alchemical process. Embrace the changes within you and trust that you are evolving into a more refined and enlightened version of yourself.

Spiritual growth: The sun's rays symbolize the spiritual and transformational process. Allow yourself to grow and evolve spiritually, trusting that the light of divine guidance is illuminating your path.

Hope and promise: The irises represent rainbows and hope, reminding you that balance and harmony bring beauty and promise into your life. Trust in the potential for positive outcomes and the fulfillment of your hopes and dreams.

Overall, the Temperance card serves as a profound reminder of the importance of balance, patience, and the alchemical transformation process. It invites you to blend different elements of your life harmoniously, trust in the gradual growth process, and embrace the spiritual journey of becoming. This card encourages you to find equilibrium, practice moderation, and trust the promise of hope and transformation.

TEMPERANCE (REVERSED)

When reversed, Temperance suggests imbalance, excess, and lack of harmony. You might be struggling to find moderation or dealing with conflicting energies, leading to stress and disharmony. This card encourages you to focus on restoring balance and integrating different aspects of your life. There could be a need to reassess your priorities and cultivate a more harmonious lifestyle. Practice patience and seek ways to create inner and outer equilibrium.

15: The Devil

CARD IMAGERY

The Devil card symbolizes control, dependency, and the darker aspects of the human psyche. The imagery on this card highlights the themes of bondage, materialism, and the shadow self.

The ram's head: Symbolizing the devil, the ram's head represents the darker forces and temptations that can lead to control and dependency. It embodies the energy of primal instincts and unchecked desires.

The chains: The chains represent control and dependency, symbolizing the emotional and material bonds that are habitual but not necessary. These chains illustrate how individuals can be trapped by their fears, addictions, and unhealthful patterns.

The lovers: The lovers are depicted as being bound by the devil's force, symbolizing how relationships and desires can become sources of entrapment and powerlessness when influenced by negative energies.

The pillars: The pillars symbolize imprisonment, representing the barriers and limitations that the Devil card signifies. They show how the shadow self can create walls restricting freedom and growth.

The black background: Depicts the darker forces or shadow self at play, symbolizing the aspects of the psyche that thrive in the absence of light and awareness.

MEANING IN A TAROT READING

When the Devil card appears in a reading, it speaks to the themes of bondage and materialism and the influence of the shadow self. It suggests that you may be facing challenges related to control, dependency, and the darker aspects of your desires and emotions.

Control and dependency: The Devil card highlights how you may feel controlled or dependent on certain habits, relationships, or material possessions. It encourages you to recognize these bonds and consider how they may limit your freedom and personal growth.

Bondage and limitation: The chains and pillars symbolize the sense of being trapped or imprisoned by your choices or circumstances. This card invites you to explore how you may be limiting yourself, and to seek liberation from these self-imposed constraints.

Shadow self: The black background and the ram's head signify the presence of darker forces or the shadow self. This card encourages you to confront these aspects of yourself honestly and with courage, understanding that acknowledging and integrating your shadow can lead to greater self-awareness and empowerment.

Unhealthful patterns: The depiction of the lovers bound by the devil's force illustrates how desires and relationships can become sources of entrapment when influenced by negative energies. This card invites you to examine your relationships and desires, seeking to transform unhealthful patterns into positive, life-affirming connections.

Awareness and liberation: The Devil card serves as a call to awareness, urging you to recognize the ways in which you may be giving away your power. By confronting and understanding these influences, you can begin the process of breaking free and reclaiming your autonomy.

The Devil card serves as a powerful reminder of the importance of recognizing and confronting the darker aspects of the human psyche. It invites you to examine how control, dependency, and the shadow self may influence your life. By acknowledging these forces, you can begin the journey toward liberation, self-awareness, and personal empowerment. This card encourages you to face your fears, break free from unhealthful patterns, and reclaim your power and freedom.

THE DEVIL (REVERSED)

Reversed, the Devil card indicates breaking free from addictions, control, and negative patterns. You may be reclaiming your power and overcoming unhealthful attachments that have been holding you back. This card suggests that you embrace liberation and personal growth. There could be a need to confront your fears and release self-imposed limitations. Focus on creating positive changes and fostering a sense of freedom.

16: The Tower

CARD IMAGERY
The Tower card symbolizes sudden upheaval, revelation, and the breakdown of existing structures. The imagery on this card highlights the themes of dramatic change, the uncovering of truth, and the need for a solid foundation.

The tower: The tower itself represents the existing structures or status quo in one's life. It symbolizes the established order, beliefs, or situations about to be challenged or transformed.

The lightning: The lightning bolt symbolizes the uncovering of truth or the revealing of previously hidden circumstances. It represents sudden insight, clarity, and the forces of change that disrupt the status quo.

The foundation: The foundation of the tower is depicted as fractured rock, symbolizing that it is not quite solid. This aspect illustrates the instability of the existing structures and the necessity for reevaluation and rebuilding.

Toppled crown: The toppled crown shows that what once was no longer exists, indicating the fall of existing structures and the loss of former status or power. It represents the dramatic and often-challenging process of dismantling the old to make way for the new.

MEANING IN A TAROT READING

When the Tower card appears in a reading, it speaks to the themes of sudden upheaval, revelation, and the need for transformation. It suggests that you may be experiencing or about to experience significant changes that will challenge your current beliefs and structures.

Sudden change and upheaval: The Tower card highlights the dramatic changes and disruptions that can occur unexpectedly. It encourages you to embrace these changes as opportunities for growth and transformation.

Revelation and insight: The lightning symbolizes the sudden insight and clarity that come with uncovering hidden truths. This card suggests that you may be faced with revelations that challenge your current understanding and prompt you to see things from a new perspective.

Instability and reevaluation: The fractured foundation indicates that the existing structures in your life may be unstable or flawed. This card invites you to reevaluate your beliefs, relationships, or situations and consider how they can be rebuilt on a more solid and authentic foundation.

Release and renewal: The toppled crown signifies the fall of old structures and the release of what no longer serves you. This card encourages you to let go of the past and embrace the process of renewal and rebuilding.

Transformation and growth: The Tower card is a powerful catalyst for transformation and growth. It reminds you that even though the process of upheaval can be challenging, it ultimately leads to greater self-awareness and resilience and a more authentic way of being.

Overall, the Tower card is a profound reminder of the necessity of sudden change and the uncovering of truth. It invites you to embrace the disruptions and revelations that challenge your existing structures, knowing they are opportunities for profound transformation and growth. This card encourages you to let go of the past, reevaluate your foundations, and rebuild on a more solid and authentic basis. Trust in the process of upheaval and renewal and welcome the new possibilities that arise from the breakdown of the old.

THE TOWER (REVERSED)
In reverse, the Tower suggests avoidance of disaster, fear of change, and delayed upheaval. You might be resisting necessary transformations or ignoring warning signs, leading to a buildup of pressure. This card encourages you to prepare for inevitable shifts and rebuild on solid foundations. There could be a need to embrace change and let go of outdated structures. Focus on resilience and adaptability to navigate through upheaval.

17: The Star

CARD IMAGERY
The Star card symbolizes hope, inspiration, and spiritual renewal. The imagery on this card highlights the themes of guidance, creativity, healing, and purity.

The eight stars: The stars represent hope and guidance, each with eight points symbolizing renewal. These stars illuminate the path forward, offering divine inspiration and a sense of direction.

The woman: The woman is a symbol of youth and creativity. She embodies the fresh energy and imaginative spirit that come with new beginnings and the pursuit of dreams.

Flowing water: Flowing water represents the water of life, symbolizing healing and fertility. It nourishes the earth and signifies the continuous flow of life and the rejuvenation of the spirit. The urns from which the water flows are extensions of this life-giving energy.

Lily: The lily symbolizes purity, representing the clarity and innocence of spiritual renewal. The lily's presence suggests a return to a state of pure potential and the blossoming of the soul.

MEANING IN A TAROT READING

When the Star card appears in a reading, it speaks to the themes of hope, inspiration, and spiritual renewal. It suggests you are entering a period of healing, creativity, and a renewed sense of purpose.

Hope and guidance: The Star card highlights the importance of hope and guidance in your life. It encourages you to trust in the divine inspiration and direction leading you toward your goals and dreams.

Renewal and inspiration: The eight-pointed stars symbolize renewal and the fresh energy of new beginnings. This card invites you to embrace your creative spirit and allow your imagination to guide you toward new possibilities.

Healing and fertility: The flowing water represents the healing and life-giving energy that nourishes your body, mind, and spirit. It suggests that you are recovering and rejuvenating, where new growth and fertility are possible.

Youth and creativity: The woman symbolizes the youthful and creative energy in your life. This card encourages you to tap into your inner creativity and express yourself authentically and joyfully.

Purity and clarity: The lily symbolizes purity and the return to clarity and innocence. It invites you to release any impurities or negativity and embrace a fresh, pure perspective on life.

The Star card is a powerful reminder of hope, inspiration, and spiritual renewal. It invites you to trust in the divine guidance leading you toward your dreams and to embrace the creative, healing energy in your life. This card encourages you to find inspiration in the beauty and purity of life and to allow your spirit to be renewed and rejuvenated. Trust in the process of healing and growth and welcome the new possibilities that arise from a place of hope and clarity.

THE STAR (REVERSED)

Reversed, the Star points to hopelessness, lack of faith, and disconnection from your inner light. You may be feeling discouraged or losing sight of your dreams, leading to a sense of despondency. This card suggests that you reconnect with your inner guidance and restore your optimism. There could be a need to cultivate hope and trust in the universe. Focus on healing and finding inspiration to reignite your aspirations.

the MOON

18: The Moon

CARD IMAGERY
The Moon card symbolizes the subconscious, intuition, and the hidden aspects of the self. The imagery on this card highlights the themes of mystery, emotional depth, and the journey into the unknown.

The moon: The moon represents night and symbolizes the subconscious and shadow self. It illuminates the hidden aspects of our psyche, revealing truths that are not visible in the light of day.

The water: Water is associated with the moon, symbolizing emotions and the subconscious. It reflects our inner world's fluid, ever-changing nature and the depths of our feelings and intuition.

The whale: Submerged and hidden from view, the whale symbolizes the need for inner work and delving into the subconscious. It represents the journey into the deep waters of the psyche to uncover hidden truths and insights.

MEANING IN A TAROT READING
When the Moon card appears in a reading, it speaks to the themes of intuition, subconscious exploration, and the hidden aspects of the self. It suggests a time for introspection and trusting your inner guidance.

Subconscious and shadow self: The Moon card highlights the importance of exploring your subconscious and understanding the shadow aspects of your personality. It encourages you to look beneath the surface and acknowledge the parts of yourself that are hidden or suppressed.

Intuition and inner guidance: This card suggests that you have heightened intuition and should trust your inner guidance. The Moon card invites you to listen to your instincts and pay attention to the subtle messages from your subconscious.

Emotional depth and fluidity: Water symbolizes the emotional and fluid nature of the subconscious mind. This card encourages you to embrace your emotions and allow yourself to feel deeply, understanding that your feelings can provide valuable insights into your inner world.

Mystery and uncertainty: The Moon card often signifies a period of mystery and uncertainty. It suggests that not everything is as it seems, and that you may need to navigate through illusions and hidden truths to find clarity.

Inner work and exploration: The submerged and hidden whale represents the need for inner work and deep exploration of the subconscious. This card encourages you to dive into the depths of your psyche, uncover hidden truths, and gain a deeper understanding of yourself.

The Moon card serves as a profound reminder of the importance of exploring the subconscious and trusting your intuition. It invites you to embrace the mystery and uncertainty of life, understanding that the hidden aspects of your psyche hold valuable insights and truths. This card encourages you to delve into the depths of your emotions, acknowledge your shadow self, and trust in the guidance of your inner wisdom. Embrace the journey into the unknown and allow the light of the moon to illuminate your path toward greater self-awareness and understanding.

THE MOON (REVERSED)

When the Moon card is reversed, it indicates confusion, illusion, and fear. You might be struggling with hidden truths or subconscious issues, leading to anxiety and uncertainty. This card suggests that you seek clarity and face your fears to illuminate the path ahead. There could be a need to confront your shadow self and bring hidden aspects to light. Focus on gaining a deeper understanding of your emotions and subconscious mind.

19: The Sun

CARD IMAGERY

The Sun card symbolizes consciousness, joy, and the illuminating power of positivity. The imagery on this card highlights themes of happiness, vitality, and the harmonious balance of inner and outer radiance.

The sun: The sun is a symbol of consciousness, joy, happiness, energy, and good health. It represents the light of awareness and the positive life force that energizes and uplifts.

Sunflower: The sunflower symbolizes growth, beauty, and strength. The sunflower's tendency to turn toward the sun illustrates the power of positivity and the nurturing effect of light and warmth.

Eight rays: The rays symbolize infinity, indicating the boundless energy and eternal nature of the sun's influence.

MEANING IN A TAROT READING

When the Sun card appears in a reading, it speaks to joy, vitality, and positive-energy themes. It suggests a time of illumination, growth, and radiant happiness.

Consciousness and clarity: The Sun card highlights the importance of awareness and clarity in your life. It encourages you to embrace the light of consciousness and to see things clearly and positively.

Joy and happiness: This card signifies a period of great joy and happiness. It invites you to bask in the warmth of positive energy and to allow yourself to experience the fullness of life's pleasures and delights.

Vitality and good health: The Sun card symbolizes vitality and good health. It suggests that you are in a state of physical and emotional well-being, filled with energy and enthusiasm for life.

Growth and beauty: The sunflower represents the growth and beauty that come from living in alignment with positive energy. This card encourages you to nurture your inner strength and to appreciate the beauty in and around you.

Radiance and harmony: The Sun card represents the ability to radiate outwardly and inwardly simultaneously. It suggests a harmonious balance where your inner light shines brightly and illuminates your external world.

Boundless energy: The eight rays symbolize infinity, indicating the boundless energy and eternal nature of the sun's influence. This card reminds you of the limitless potential within you and the infinite possibilities that life offers.

Overall, the Sun card is a powerful reminder of the importance of joy, positivity, and radiant energy in your life. It invites you to embrace the light of consciousness, experience the fullness of joy and happiness, and radiate your positive energy inwardly and outwardly. This card encourages you to appreciate the growth and beauty of living in alignment with your true self and to trust in life's boundless energy and infinite possibilities. Allow the sun's light to illuminate your path and fill your life with warmth, vitality, and happiness.

THE SUN (REVERSED)
Reversed, the Sun card suggests temporary setbacks, lack of enthusiasm, and hidden difficulties. You may be experiencing delays or feeling less optimistic, leading to a sense of discouragement. This card encourages you to find the silver lining and restore your vitality. There could be a need to address underlying issues and reignite your passion. Focus on positive thinking and creating opportunities for joy and success.

20: Judgement

CARD IMAGERY
The Judgement card symbolizes awakening, illumination, and the call to rise above past limitations. The imagery on this card highlights themes of rebirth, important decisions, and the divine call to action.

Angel wings: The angel wings symbolize archangel Gabriel; the wings represent awakening. Gabriel, known as the bearer of important news, calls us to higher awareness and spiritual rebirth, much like when he announced to Mary that she would be the mother of God.

The sun: The sun is a symbol of illumination and resurrection. It represents the clarity and enlightenment that come with a spiritual awakening, shedding light on the path to renewal and new beginnings.

Sapling: This represents new life, symbolizing the fresh start and growth that result from heeding the call to transformation and leaving the past behind.

Trumpet: The trumpet's call signifies the time to resurrect the past and make a decisive choice. It also references fame, suggesting a moment of recognition and the call to step into the spotlight of your true purpose.

MEANING IN A TAROT READING

When the Judgement card appears in a reading, it speaks to the themes of awakening, transformation, and decisive action. It suggests a call to rise above past limitations and embrace a higher purpose.

Awakening and renewal: The Judgement card highlights the importance of awakening to a new level of consciousness. It encourages you to embrace the process of spiritual rebirth and to let go of past burdens that no longer serve you.

Illumination and clarity: The sun symbolizes the illumination that comes with awakening. This card suggests that you are gaining clarity and insight into your true path and purpose, guiding you toward a brighter future.

New beginnings: The new plant represents the potential for new life and growth. This card invites you to nurture new opportunities and embrace the fresh start that comes with leaving the past behind.

Call to action: The trumpet signifies the call to take decisive action and make important decisions that will shape your future. It urges you to heed your inner voice's call and step into the spotlight of your true potential.

Recognition and fame: The trumpet also references fame, suggesting that your efforts and transformations may lead to recognition and acknowledgment from others. Embrace the opportunities for growth and success that come your way.

The Judgement card is a powerful reminder of the importance of awakening, transformation, and decisive action in your life. It invites you to rise above past limitations, embrace a higher purpose, and step into the light of your true potential. This card encourages you to listen to your inner voice's call, make crucial decisions with clarity and confidence, and welcome the new beginnings and growth that come from a spiritual awakening. Trust in the process of illumination and resurrection and allow the divine guidance of archangel Gabriel to lead you toward a brighter, more fulfilling future.

JUDGEMENT (REVERSED)
In reverse, the Judgement card points to self-doubt, lack of closure, and refusal to learn from past mistakes. You may be avoiding important decisions or feeling stuck, leading to stagnation. This card suggests that you reflect on your actions, seek forgiveness, and embrace personal growth. There could be a need to confront your past and make amends. Focus on self-awareness and taking responsibility for your choices.

21: The World

CARD IMAGERY
The World card symbolizes completion, fulfillment, and the culmination of a journey. The imagery on this card highlights themes of wholeness, integration, and the cyclical nature of life.

Symbols of the Minor Arcana: All the symbols of the Minor Arcana are fully revealed, unlike with the Fool, where they were obscured by roots. This signifies the mastery and integration of all elements and aspects of life. The Fool's journey has come full circle.

Ouroboros: The ouroboros indicates that things have come full circle, marking the end of a journey. It represents the eternal cycle of life, death, and rebirth, indicating the completion and renewal inherent in all things.

The fish: The fish represents the salmon's journey to spawn, symbolizing a great adventure that also comes full circle. It embodies the concept of returning to one's origins after a transformative journey.

White flower: The white flower references the Fool, signifying that what was present at the beginning is also present at the end. It symbolizes purity, innocence, and the continuous cycle of beginnings and endings.

The fish and the flower: These symbols represent the sea and the earth, symbolizing the harmony and balance between different elements and realms.

Contrast between light and dark: The Fool was light, and the World is dark, symbolizing the beginning and end of a journey. This contrast underscores the duality and completeness of the cycle of life.

MEANING IN A TAROT READING

When the World card appears in a reading, it speaks to the themes of completion, fulfillment, and the successful culmination of a journey. It suggests that you have reached a point of wholeness and integration in your life.

Completion and fulfillment: The World card highlights the importance of recognizing and celebrating the completion of a significant journey. It encourages you to acknowledge your achievements and the sense of fulfillment that comes with reaching your goals.

Wholeness and integration: This card signifies the integration of all aspects of your life, symbolized by the fully revealed symbols of the Minor Arcana. It suggests that you have mastered the lessons and experiences of your journey, leading to a sense of wholeness and balance.

Cyclical nature of life: The ouroboros and the fish symbolize the cyclical nature of life, reminding you that endings are also beginnings. This card invites you to embrace the continuous cycle of transformation and renewal.

Return to origins: The fish's journey to spawn and the white flower, referencing the Fool, indicate a return to origins after a transformative adventure. This card encourages you to reflect on how far you've come and recognize the continuous growth and change thread.

Harmony and balance: The fish and the flower represent the sea and the earth, symbolizing the balance between different elements and realms. This card suggests that you have successfully integrated various aspects of your life.

Duality and completeness: The contrast between light and dark symbolizes the beginning and end of a journey, highlighting the duality and completeness of the cycle of life. This card invites you to embrace both the light and dark aspects of your journey and recognize all experiences' interconnectedness.

Overall, the World card serves as a profound reminder of the importance of completion, fulfillment, and the cyclical nature of life. It invites you to celebrate your journey's successful culmination, recognize the wholeness and integration you have achieved, and embrace the continuous cycle of beginnings and endings. This card encourages you to reflect on your growth, acknowledge the harmony and balance in your life, and understand that every ending is also a new beginning. Trust in the completeness of your journey and welcome the renewal and transformation that come with each life cycle.

THE WORLD (REVERSED)
Reversed, the World indicates incomplete cycles, lack of closure, and feeling unfulfilled. You may be struggling to achieve your goals or finish what you started, leading to a sense of dissatisfaction. This card suggests that you focus on tying up loose ends and embracing new opportunities. There could be a need to reassess your objectives and create a sense of completion. Focus on celebrating your achievements and preparing for the next phase.

THE
MINOR ARCANA

THE SUIT OF WANDS

Ace *of* Wands

MEANING IN A TAROT READING

When the Ace of Wands appears in a reading, it is a powerful symbol of new beginnings, creativity, and the spark of inspiration. This card urges you to act on your ideas and embrace the dynamic energy of starting something new.

Action on ideas: The mantra of this card, "Action on ideas," highlights the importance of moving forward with your creative thoughts and plans. It encourages you to take the first step and to trust in your ability to bring your ideas to life. The energy of the Ace of Wands is about igniting the fire within and using it to fuel your ambitions.

New beginnings: The Ace of Wands signifies a fresh start and the potential for new ventures. It suggests that now is the time to pursue your passions and explore new opportunities enthusiastically and confidently. This card embodies the spirit of initiation and the excitement that comes with embarking on a new journey.

Creative energy: This card is a beacon of creative energy and inspiration. It encourages you to tap into your inner creativity and to use your imagination to fuel your projects and ambitions. The Ace of Wands symbolizes the birth of ideas and the courage to pursue them with vigor.

Leadership and independence: With the influence of the number one, the Ace of Wands emphasizes the importance of taking the lead and being independent. The number one in numerology is associated with leadership, initiative, and self-reliance. This card encourages you to trust in your abilities and to confidently step into a position of leadership in your pursuits.

Divine inspiration: The Ace of Wands suggests that your ideas are divinely inspired and supported by the universe. It indicates that you are being guided and that your creative impulses are aligned with a higher purpose. This card reminds you to stay open to inspiration and to follow the path that feels most authentic to you.

Passion and enthusiasm: The Ace of Wands represents the passion and enthusiasm that drive you to act. It reminds you to harness this energy and let it propel you with vigor and determination toward your goals. This card is about embracing the excitement and potential of new beginnings and using that energy to create positive change.

NUMEROLOGICAL SIGNIFICANCE

In numerology, the number one is associated with new beginnings, independence, and leadership. It represents the starting point of a new journey and the potential to carve out your own path with confidence and determination. The Ace of Wands, as the first card in the suit of Wands, embodies these qualities and emphasizes the importance of taking initiative and embracing your individuality.

New beginnings: The number one is the starting point, representing new beginnings and the birth of ideas. The Ace of Wands encourages you to embrace these new beginnings with enthusiasm and to take the first step toward your goals.

Independence: The number one symbolizes independence and self-reliance. The Ace of Wands encourages you to trust in your abilities and to take charge of your creative endeavors with confidence.

Leadership: The number one is also associated with leadership and initiative. The Ace of Wands reminds you to take the lead in your projects and to inspire others with your vision and passion.

The Ace of Wands is a card of dynamic energy, creativity, and new beginnings. It encourages you to act on your ideas, embrace the potential for growth, and trust in your ability to lead and create. This card serves as a reminder that the universe supports you and that now is the time to pursue your passions with enthusiasm and confidence.

ACE OF WANDS REVERSED

Blocked creativity: You may feel a surge of ideas but find it difficult to channel them into something productive. Creative blocks can stem from self-doubt or external pressures.

Delayed beginnings: Projects and new ventures may be slowed by unforeseen obstacles. This could involve logistical issues, lack of resources, or misalignment with timing.

Lack of direction: There is a sense of aimlessness, making it hard to focus on a clear path. This can lead to hesitation and second-guessing your choices.

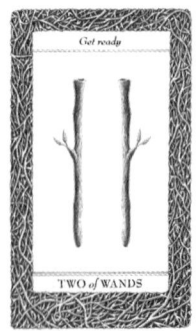

Two of Wands

MEANING IN A TAROT READING

When the Two of Wands appears in a reading, it signifies preparation, foresight, and planning for the future. This card embodies the energy of anticipation and readiness for what lies ahead. It encourages you to step back, assess your situation, and make informed decisions to ensure your success.

Get ready: This card's mantra, "Get ready," highlights the importance of preparation and planning. It suggests that now is the time to gather your resources, set your goals, and lay the groundwork for future endeavors. This card is about being proactive and strategic in your approach.

Foresight and vision: The Two of Wands represents the ability to see the bigger picture and to anticipate what is needed to achieve your goals. It encourages you to think ahead, consider all possibilities, and make decisions that align with your long-term vision. This card is about foresight to plan and prepare for the future.

Strategic planning: This card emphasizes the importance of strategic planning and careful consideration. It suggests that you evaluate your options, weigh the pros and cons, and develop a clear plan of action. The Two of Wands reminds you that successful outcomes are often the result of thorough preparation and thoughtful planning.

Balancing options: The Two of Wands often involves a decision between two paths or options. It encourages you to carefully consider your choices and to ensure that they align with your goals and values. This card is about finding balance and making decisions that support your overall vision.

Ambition and aspiration: The Two of Wands signifies ambition and the desire to expand your horizons. It encourages you to set high goals for yourself and to pursue them with determination and confidence. This card is about having the ambition to reach beyond your current circumstances and to strive for greater success.

NUMEROLOGICAL SIGNIFICANCE

In numerology, the number two is associated with balance, partnerships, and duality. It represents the need to harmonize different aspects of one's life and to find equilibrium in one's decisions and actions. The Two of Wands, the second card in the suit of Wands, embodies these qualities and emphasizes the importance of preparation and collaboration.

Balance: The number two signifies the need for balance and harmony. The Two of Wands encourages you to balance your plans and aspirations with practical considerations and to ensure that your decisions are well rounded and thoughtful.

Partnerships: The number two also represents partnerships and collaboration. The Two of Wands suggests that working with others and seeking input from trusted advisors can enhance your planning process and lead to better outcomes.

Duality: The number two highlights the duality of choices and options. The Two of Wands reminds you to carefully consider all possibilities and to make decisions that are aligned with your long-term vision and goals.

The Two of Wands is a card of preparation, foresight, and strategic planning. It encourages you to prepare for what lies ahead by gathering your resources, setting clear goals, and making informed decisions. This card serves as a reminder that successful outcomes are often the result of careful planning and thoughtful consideration. Embrace the energy of anticipation and readiness, and trust in your ability to navigate the path ahead with confidence and clarity.

TWO OF WANDS REVERSED

Fear of change: You might be holding back from exploring new opportunities due to fear of the unknown. This can lead to missed chances and stagnation.

Indecision: Important decisions are challenging, and there's a struggle to commit to a course of action. This often results in procrastination and wasted potential.

Limited perspective: Being overly focused on immediate concerns prevents you from seeing the broader picture, which limits growth and opportunities.

Three *of* Wands

MEANING IN A TAROT READING

When the Three of Wands appears in a reading, it signifies progress, expansion, and the readiness to take action. This card embodies the energy of moving forward with confidence and anticipation of success. It encourages you to embrace the opportunities that lie ahead and to pursue your goals actively.

Ready, set, go: This card's mantra, "Ready, set, go," highlights the importance of being prepared and taking decisive action. It suggests that you are now ready to move forward with your plans and embark on new ventures with enthusiasm and determination.

Expansion and growth: The Three of Wands represents the expansion of horizons and the pursuit of new opportunities. It encourages you to look beyond your current situation and explore new growth and development possibilities. This card is about seeking out new experiences and pushing the boundaries of what is possible.

Forward momentum: This card signifies forward momentum and the drive to achieve your goals. It suggests that you are on the right path and that your efforts are beginning to bear fruit. The Three of Wands reminds you to maintain your focus and keep pushing ahead confidently.

Taking action: The Three of Wands emphasizes the importance of taking action and making progress. It encourages you to seize the opportunities that come your way and to pursue your ambitions actively. This card is about being proactive and taking the necessary steps to achieve your desired outcomes.

Vision and planning: This card also highlights the importance of having a clear vision and a well-thought-out plan. It suggests that your success results from careful planning and strategic thinking. The Three of Wands reminds you to focus on your long-term goals and continue working toward them with determination.

NUMEROLOGICAL SIGNIFICANCE
In numerology, the number three is associated with creativity, communication, and expansion. It represents the

growth of combining ideas and energies to create something new. The Three of Wands, as the third card in the suit of Wands, embodies these qualities and emphasizes the importance of moving forward and taking action.

Creativity: The number three signifies creativity and the ability to generate new ideas. The Three of Wands encourages you to tap into your creative potential and to use it to drive your progress and success.

Communication: The number three also represents communication and collaboration. The Three of Wands suggests that working with others and sharing your vision can enhance your efforts and lead to greater success.

Expansion: The number three highlights the theme of expansion and growth. The Three of Wands encourages you to seek out new opportunities and to embrace the possibilities for growth and development that lie ahead.

The Three of Wands is a card of progress, expansion, and action. It encourages you to move forward with confidence, to embrace new opportunities, and to actively pursue your goals. This card serves as a reminder that you are ready to take the next steps and that your efforts are beginning to pay off. Embrace the energy of "Ready, set, go" and trust in your ability to achieve success through determination, vision, and action.

THREE OF WANDS REVERSED

Setbacks: Plans may face unexpected delays or failures, causing frustration. It's important to reassess and adapt rather than abandon your efforts.

Lack of foresight: Neglecting to plan ahead leads to avoidable problems. Ensure that you're considering future implications of your actions.

Disappointment: Despite hard work, the outcomes may not meet expectations, leading to disillusionment. Reflect on what can be learned from these experiences.

Four *of* Wands

MEANING IN A TAROT READING
When the Four of Wands appears in a reading, it signifies foundation, stability, and celebrating achievements. This card embodies the energy of solidifying your efforts and enjoying the rewards of your hard work. It encourages you to appreciate the stability you have created and to build upon it for future growth.

Foundation and stability: The mantra of this card, "Foundation and stability," highlights the importance of creating a solid base in your life. It suggests that now is the time to acknowledge the strong foundations you have built, and to ensure they are secure and enduring.

Celebration and achievement: The Four of Wands represents the joy and satisfaction of achieving your goals. It encourages you to celebrate your successes and take pride in your progress. This card is about recognizing and appreciating the milestones you have reached.

Community and support: This card signifies the importance of community and support. The stability you seek is often strengthened by your connections and relationships with others. The Four of Wands reminds you to appreciate the support of those around you and to celebrate your achievements together.

Harmony and balance: The Four of Wands emphasizes the need for harmony and balance in your life. It encourages you to create a stable environment to thrive and grow. This card is about finding equilibrium and maintaining a sense of peace and contentment.

Building for the future: This card also highlights the importance of laying the groundwork for future success. The stability you create now will serve as a strong foundation for future endeavors. The Four of Wands reminds you to focus on long-term stability and to build upon your current achievements.

NUMEROLOGICAL SIGNIFICANCE

In numerology, the number four is associated with stability, structure, and foundation. It represents the solid base upon which future growth can be built. The Four of Wands, as the fourth card in the suit of Wands, embodies these qualities and emphasizes the importance of creating a stable and secure foundation.

Stability: The number four signifies stability and the need for a solid foundation. The Four of Wands encourages you to focus on creating a stable environment in your life, where you can feel secure and supported.

Structure: The number four also represents structure and order. The Four of Wands suggests that establishing clear structures and routines can enhance your sense of stability and help you achieve your goals.

Foundation: The number four highlights the importance of a strong foundation. The Four of Wands reminds you that the stability you create now will support your future growth and success.

The Four of Wands is a card of foundation, stability, and celebration. It encourages you to acknowledge and appreciate the strong foundations you have built, and to celebrate your achievements. This card serves as a reminder that stability and support are essential for future growth and success. Embrace the energy of "Foundation and stability" and trust in your ability to create a secure and harmonious environment where you can thrive.

FOUR OF WANDS REVERSED

Disruption: Celebratory events or milestones might be marred by conflict or unexpected issues. This can dampen the joy and satisfaction normally associated with achievements.

Unstable foundations: Relationships or projects built on shaky ground may reveal cracks. It's crucial to address these issues to ensure long-term stability.

Delayed gratification: Successes are postponed, requiring patience and perseverance. Use this time to strengthen your foundation and resolve.

Five *of* Wands

MEANING IN A TAROT READING

When the Five of Wands appears in a reading, it signifies competition, rivalry, and the challenges that come with vying for a position. This card embodies the energy of dynamic interaction and the need to assert oneself in the face of opposition. It encourages you to embrace the competitive spirit and to use it as a catalyst for growth and improvement.

Competition: The mantra of this card, "Competition," highlights the importance of recognizing and engaging in competitive situations. It suggests that you are in an environment where rivalry and the struggle for dominance are prevalent. This card is about understanding the nature of competition and navigating it effectively.

Rivalry and conflict: The Five of Wands represents the presence of rivalry and conflict. It encourages you to be aware of the challenges posed by others and to prepare yourself to meet them head on. This card is about standing your ground and asserting your position with confidence.

Vying for position: This card signifies the struggle to attain a higher position or to be recognized for your efforts. It suggests that you may need to compete with others to achieve your goals. The Five of Wands reminds you that competition can be a driving force that pushes you to excel and improve.

Dynamic interaction: The Five of Wands emphasizes the importance of dynamic interaction and the exchange of ideas and strategies. It encourages you to engage with others, to understand their perspectives, and to use this interaction to refine your approach. This card is about learning from the competition and using it to enhance your skills and strategies.

Overcoming challenges: This card also highlights the necessity of overcoming challenges and obstacles. It suggests that the path to success may be fraught with difficulties, but with determination and perseverance, you can prevail. The Five of Wands reminds you to stay focused and resilient in the face of adversity.

NUMEROLOGICAL SIGNIFICANCE

In numerology, the number five is associated with change, challenge, and conflict. It represents the dynamic and often-disruptive energy that prompts growth and transformation. The Five of Wands, as the fifth card in the suit of Wands, embodies these qualities and emphasizes the importance of competition and the challenges it brings.

Change: The number five signifies change and the upheaval accompanying it. The Five of Wands encourages you to embrace the changes that competition brings and to see them as opportunities for growth.

Challenge: The number five also represents challenge and conflict. The Five of Wands suggests that you are in a phase where challenges are prominent, and it is essential to face them with courage and determination.

Dynamic energy: The number five highlights the dynamic and often-unpredictable nature of life. The Five of Wands reminds you to be adaptable and to use the energy of competition to propel yourself forward.

The Five of Wands is a card of competition, rivalry, and the challenges that come with vying for position. It encourages you to recognize your environment's competitive dynamics and engage with them proactively. This card serves as a reminder that competition can be a powerful motivator for growth and improvement. Embrace the energy of "Competition" and trust in your ability to navigate rivalry and conflict with confidence and resilience.

FIVE OF WANDS REVERSED

Avoiding conflict: A desire to steer clear of disputes can lead to unresolved issues festering. Confronting problems directly may be necessary to find peace.

Inner struggle: Internal conflicts and self-doubt create emotional turmoil. It's important to address these inner battles to find clarity and confidence.

Compromise: Reaching a middle ground can resolve disputes but may require sacrifices. Ensure that compromises do not undermine your core values.

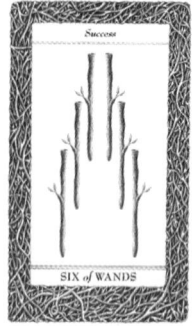

Six *of* Wands

MEANING IN A TAROT READING

When the Six of Wands appears in a reading, it signifies success, victory, and public recognition. This card embodies the energy of achievement and the accolades that come with it. However, it also serves as a reminder to remain humble and grounded, as the journey toward ultimate success is ongoing.

Success: The mantra of this card, "Success," highlights the importance of acknowledging and celebrating your achievements. It suggests that you have reached a significant milestone and that your efforts are being recognized and rewarded. This card is about enjoying the fruits of your labor and taking pride in your accomplishments.

Victory and recognition: The Six of Wands represents victory and public recognition. It encourages you to embrace the praise and acknowledgment you receive and to use it as motivation to continue striving for excellence. This card is about being seen and appreciated for your contributions.

Midway point: This card signifies that while you have achieved a notable victory, it is also a midway point in your journey. It suggests that there is still more work to be done and more challenges to overcome. The Six of Wands reminds you to stay focused and committed to your long-term goals.

Humility: The Six of Wands emphasizes the importance of humility in the face of success. It encourages you to remain grounded and to recognize that your achievements are part of a larger journey. This card is about balancing pride in your accomplishments with the awareness that there is always room for growth and improvement.

Inspiration to others: This card also highlights your role as an inspiration to others. Your success can serve as a beacon of hope and motivation for those around you. The Six of Wands reminds you to share your victories and to support and uplift others on their journeys.

NUMEROLOGICAL SIGNIFICANCE

In numerology, the number six is associated with harmony, balance, and responsibility. It represents the need to find equilibrium between different aspects of life and to fulfill one's duties with integrity. The Six of Wands, as the sixth card in the suit of Wands, embodies these qualities and emphasizes the importance of balanced success and humility.

Harmony: The number six signifies harmony and balance. The Six of Wands encourages you to find a balance between celebrating your success and staying humble. It reminds you to maintain harmony in your relationships and interactions with others, even in times of victory.

Responsibility: The number six also represents responsibility. The Six of Wands suggests that with success comes the responsibility to use your influence and recognition wisely. It encourages you to act with integrity and to support others in their pursuits.

Balance: The number six highlights the importance of balance. The Six of Wands reminds you to balance your pride in your achievements with the awareness of your ongoing journey and the need for continuous growth.

The Six of Wands is a card of success, victory, and public recognition. It encourages you to celebrate your achievements and take pride in them. However, it also serves as a reminder to remain humble and grounded, recognizing that success is a journey with ongoing challenges and opportunities for growth. Embrace the energy of "Success" and use your victory as motivation to continue striving for excellence while inspiring and supporting others along the way.

SIX OF WANDS REVERSED

Lack of recognition: Efforts go unnoticed, causing feelings of being undervalued. Seek validation within yourself and from supportive peers.

Self-doubt: Questioning your worth and abilities can hinder progress. Build self-esteem by recognizing your achievements, however small.

False victory: Success might be superficial or not as fulfilling as expected. Reflect on what true success means to you, and aim for deeper satisfaction.

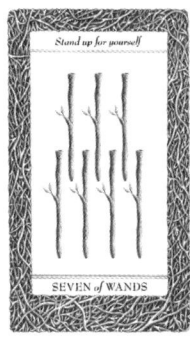

Seven *of* Wands

MEANING IN A TAROT READING

When the Seven of Wands appears in a reading, it signifies the need to defend yourself, your beliefs, or your position. This card embodies the energy of standing up for yourself, even in the face of adversity or when you feel ill prepared. It encourages you to hold your ground and assert your values and principles with courage and determination.

Stand up for yourself: The mantra of this card, "Stand up for yourself," highlights the importance of defending your beliefs and positions. It suggests that you may be facing challenges or opposition and that it is crucial to remain firm and resolute. This card is about having the courage to protect what is important to you.

Defending beliefs: The Seven of Wands represents the struggle to defend your beliefs or position against external pressures. It encourages you to stay true to your values and to resist any attempts to undermine or discredit you. This card is about being steadfast in your convictions, even when it feels difficult.

Courage in adversity: This card signifies the need for courage in the face of adversity. It suggests that you may feel outnumbered or ill prepared, but it is essential to confront challenges head on. The Seven of Wands reminds you that standing up for yourself requires bravery and perseverance.

Overcoming obstacles: The Seven of Wands emphasizes the importance of overcoming obstacles and challenges. It encourages you to see these difficulties as opportunities to strengthen your resolve and to prove your commitment to your beliefs. This card is about rising to the occasion and demonstrating your inner strength.

Resilience: This card also highlights the need for resilience. It suggests that you may encounter setbacks or resistance, but it is crucial to keep pushing forward. The Seven of Wands reminds you that resilience and determination are key to defending your position and achieving success.

NUMEROLOGICAL SIGNIFICANCE

In numerology, the number seven is associated with introspection, wisdom, and perseverance. It represents the quest for deeper understanding and the strength to endure challenges. The Seven of Wands, as the seventh card in the suit of Wands, embodies these qualities and emphasizes the importance of standing up for yourself and defending your beliefs.

Introspection: The number seven signifies introspection and the search for deeper meaning. The Seven of Wands encourages you to reflect on your values and principles and to understand why they are worth defending. It reminds you to draw strength from your inner convictions.

Wisdom: The number seven also represents wisdom. The Seven of Wands suggests that standing up for yourself requires not only courage but also wisdom. It encourages you to approach challenges with a clear mind and a thoughtful strategy.

Perseverance: The number seven highlights the importance of perseverance. The Seven of Wands reminds you that defending your position often involves enduring difficulties and setbacks. It encourages you to remain steadfast and to persist in the face of adversity.

The Seven of Wands is a card of defense, courage, and resilience. It encourages you to stand up for yourself, your beliefs, and your position, even when faced with challenges or opposition. This card serves as a reminder that defending your values requires courage, wisdom, and perseverance. Embrace the energy of "Stand up for yourself" and trust in your ability to protect what is important to you with determination and strength.

SEVEN OF WANDS REVERSED

Overwhelmed: Feeling outnumbered or outmatched by challenges can lead to a sense of defeat. Prioritize your battles and seek support when needed.

Defensiveness: Overreacting to criticism can create tension in relationships. Strive for constructive feedback and avoid taking things personally.

Giving up: A lack of resilience in the face of obstacles may tempt you to quit. Reconnect with your purpose and find ways to reenergize your efforts.

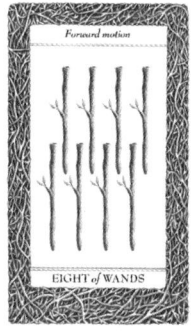

Eight *of* Wands

MEANING IN A TAROT READING

When the Eight of Wands appears in a reading, it signifies rapid progress, forward motion, and the swift movement of events. This card embodies the energy of momentum and the absence of setbacks or delays. It encourages you to embrace the flow of progress and move confidently toward your goals.

Forward motion: The mantra of this card, "Forward motion," highlights the importance of continual progress and movement. It suggests that things are advancing quickly and that you are on a path of rapid development. This card is about harnessing the momentum and riding the wave of progress.

Rapid progress: The Eight of Wands represents the swift movement and rapid advancement of your plans and projects. It encourages you to stay focused and to capitalize on the speed at which things are unfolding. This card is about making the most of the opportunities that come your way.

Momentum: This card signifies the power of momentum and the acceleration of events. It suggests that once you set things in motion, they will continue to progress with little resistance. The Eight of Wands reminds you that momentum is on your side, and it is essential to maintain your pace.

No setbacks or delays: The Eight of Wands emphasizes the absence of setbacks or delays. It encourages you to trust that your efforts will yield positive results without unnecessary hindrances. This card is about moving forward smoothly and efficiently toward your goals.

Clear communication: This card also highlights the importance of clear and direct communication. It suggests that messages and information are being conveyed swiftly and effectively. The Eight of Wands reminds you that clear communication can facilitate progress and prevent misunderstandings.

NUMEROLOGICAL SIGNIFICANCE

In numerology, the number eight is associated with power, efficiency, and balance. It represents the ability to achieve goals through focused effort and the effective use of resources. The Eight of Wands, as the eighth card in the suit of Wands, embodies these qualities and emphasizes the importance of forward motion and rapid progress.

Power and efficiency: The number eight signifies power and efficiency. The Eight of Wands encourages you to use your energy and resources effectively to achieve your goals. It reminds you that efficiency and focused effort can lead to swift progress.

Balance: The number eight also represents balance. The Eight of Wands suggests that maintaining a balanced approach can help you navigate the rapid movement of events. It encourages you to stay grounded and focused, even as things progress quickly.

Achievement: The number eight highlights the potential for achievement. The Eight of Wands reminds you that forward motion and rapid progress can lead to significant accomplishments. It encourages you to embrace the momentum and to trust in your ability to succeed.

The Eight of Wands is a card of rapid progress, forward motion, and the absence of setbacks or delays. It encourages you to embrace the swift movement of events and to capitalize on the momentum. This card serves as a reminder that things are progressing smoothly and that you are on a path of swift advancement. Embrace the energy of "Forward motion" and trust in your ability to achieve your goals efficiently and effectively.

EIGHT OF WANDS REVERSED

Delays: Progress is hindered by unexpected setbacks. Patience and flexibility are essential to navigate these interruptions.

Miscommunication: Messages are misunderstood or lost in translation, leading to confusion. Clear and concise communication can mitigate these issues.

Hasty decisions: Rushing into actions without proper planning can lead to mistakes. Take time to consider all angles before proceeding.

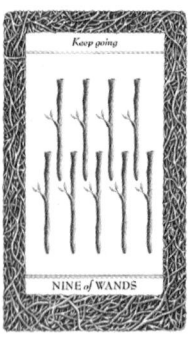

Nine *of* Wands

MEANING IN A TAROT READING

When the Nine of Wands appears in a reading, it signifies perseverance, resilience, and the determination to achieve your goals despite challenges. This card embodies the energy of persistence and the importance of continuing your efforts as you near the finish line. It encourages you to keep going, even when the journey has been tough, since success is within reach.

Keep going: The mantra of this card, "Keep going," highlights the importance of perseverance and resilience. It suggests that you are close to achieving your goals, and it is crucial to maintain your efforts. This card is about pushing through difficulties and staying committed to your path.

Nearly there: The Nine of Wands represents being on the verge of completing a significant phase or reaching a major milestone. It encourages you to recognize how far you have come and to stay focused as you approach your goal. This card is about the final push and the determination to see things through to the end.

Resilience and strength: This card signifies the need for resilience and inner strength. It suggests that you have faced challenges and obstacles but have the strength to overcome them. The Nine of Wands reminds you that your hard work and perseverance will pay off.

Persistence: The Nine of Wands emphasizes the importance of persistence. It encourages you to keep moving forward, even when you feel tired or discouraged. This card is about maintaining your resolve and working toward your objectives.

Guarding your progress: This card also highlights the need to protect and defend the progress you have made. It suggests that you may need to stand your ground and safeguard your achievements. The Nine of Wands reminds you to stay vigilant and to ensure that your hard work is not undermined.

NUMEROLOGICAL SIGNIFICANCE

In numerology, the number nine is associated with completion, fulfillment, and the culmination of efforts. It represents the final stages of a journey and the nearing of completion. The Nine of Wands, as the ninth card in the suit of Wands, embodies these qualities and emphasizes the importance of perseverance and resilience as you approach your goals.

Completion: The number nine signifies completion and the culmination of efforts. The Nine of Wands encourages you to recognize that you are nearing the end of a significant phase and to stay focused on your final push toward success.

Fulfillment: The number nine also represents fulfillment. The Nine of Wands suggests that your hard work and persistence will lead to a sense of accomplishment and fulfillment. It reminds you that your efforts are bringing you closer to achieving your goals.

Culmination: The number nine highlights the culmination of a journey. The Nine of Wands reminds you that you are in the final stages of your efforts, and that it is essential to stay committed and resilient as you approach the finish line.

The Nine of Wands is a card of perseverance, resilience, and determination. It encourages you to keep going and to stay focused on your goals, even when faced with challenges. This card serves as a reminder that you are nearly there, and that your hard work and persistence will pay off. Embrace the energy of "Keep going" and trust in your ability to achieve your goals through resilience and determination.

NINE OF WANDS REVERSED

Exhaustion: Overwhelmed by ongoing struggles, you may feel too tired to continue. It's important to rest and recharge to avoid burnout.

Paranoia: Unjustified fear of being attacked or criticized creates unnecessary stress. Focus on reality and avoid letting anxiety dictate your actions.

Vulnerability: Feeling exposed and insecure can weaken your defenses. Build emotional resilience and seek support from trusted allies.

Ten *of* Wands

MEANING IN A TAROT READING

When the Ten of Wands appears in a reading, it signifies burden, pressure, and the weight of responsibilities. This card embodies the energy of carrying a heavy load and the challenges that come with being under pressure. It encourages you to acknowledge the burdens you are carrying and to find ways to lighten your load or manage your responsibilities more effectively.

The uphill struggle: The mantra of this card, "The uphill struggle," highlights the importance of recognizing the difficulties and pressures you are facing. It suggests that you are carrying a significant burden and that the journey feels arduous. This card is about understanding the weight of your responsibilities and the need to address them.

Under pressure: The Ten of Wands represents the feeling of being under intense pressure. It encourages you to acknowledge the stress and strain you are experiencing and to find ways to manage it. This card is about recognizing the impact of carrying too much and the importance of seeking relief.

Carrying a burden: This card signifies the weight of carrying a heavy burden. It suggests that you have taken on a lot of responsibilities or challenges, and it is essential to consider whether you can sustain this load. The Ten of Wands reminds you to evaluate your commitments and to delegate or release what you can.

Completion and feeling overwhelmed: The Ten of Wands emphasizes the theme of completion and the feeling of being overwhelmed as you approach the end of a significant phase. It encourages you to push through despite the difficulties, knowing that the end is in sight. This card is about persevering through the final, challenging stages.

Managing responsibilities: This card also highlights the importance of managing your responsibilities effectively. It suggests that you need to find balance and prioritize your tasks to avoid burnout. The Ten of Wands reminds you to seek support and to share the load where possible.

NUMEROLOGICAL SIGNIFICANCE

In numerology, the number ten is associated with completion, fulfillment, and the end of a cycle. It represents the culmination of efforts and the transition to a new beginning. The Ten of Wands, as the tenth card in the suit of Wands, embodies these qualities and emphasizes the importance of managing burdens and responsibilities as you approach the completion of a significant phase.

Completion: The number ten signifies completion and the end of a cycle. The Ten of Wands encourages you to recognize that you are nearing the end of a challenging journey and to stay focused on reaching the finish line.

Fulfillment: The number ten also represents fulfillment. The Ten of Wands suggests that despite the burdens you are carrying, you are moving toward a sense of accomplishment and fulfillment. It reminds you that your efforts will ultimately pay off.

Transition: The number ten highlights the theme of transition. The Ten of Wands reminds you that the challenges you are facing are part of a larger process of growth and change. It encourages you to stay resilient as you navigate this transition.

The Ten of Wands is a card of burden, pressure, and the uphill struggle. It encourages you to acknowledge the weight of your responsibilities and to find ways to manage them effectively. This card serves as a reminder that while you are under pressure, you are also nearing the completion of a significant phase. Embrace the energy of "The uphill struggle" and trust in your ability to persevere and manage your burdens as you approach the end of your journey.

TEN OF WANDS REVERSED

Burnout: Overburdened by responsibilities, it's crucial to delegate tasks and lighten your load. Self-care is essential to maintain balance.

Refusing help: Insisting on handling everything alone can lead to unnecessary stress. Accepting assistance can alleviate pressure and foster collaboration.

Letting go: Release burdens that are not yours to carry, focusing on what truly matters. This can lead to a sense of liberation and clarity.

Page *of* Wands

MEANING IN A TAROT READING

When the Page of Wands appears in a reading, it signifies newness, creativity, and the enthusiastic expression of ideas. This card embodies the energy of youthful exuberance and the excitement of embarking on new creative ventures. It encourages you to embrace your creative potential and explore new opportunities with curiosity and enthusiasm.

Creative expression: The mantra of this card, "Creative expression," highlights the importance of embracing your creativity and finding new ways to express yourself. It suggests that you are on the brink of a new creative journey, and that it is time to explore your ideas with passion and excitement.

Newness: The Page of Wands represents the beginning of new ventures and creative projects. It encourages you to approach these opportunities with a fresh perspective and an open mind. This card is about welcoming the new and being open to the possibilities that come with it.

Youthful enthusiasm: This card signifies youthful enthusiasm and the excitement of starting something new. It suggests that you tap into your inner child and approach your projects with a sense of wonder and curiosity. The Page of Wands reminds you that a playful and adventurous spirit can lead to innovative and creative outcomes.

Exploration and adventure: The Page of Wands emphasizes the importance of exploration and adventure in the creative process. It encourages you to step out of your comfort zone and to try new things. This card is about taking risks and being willing to explore uncharted territory in your creative pursuits.

Inspiration and potential: This card also highlights the themes of inspiration and potential. It suggests that you are filled with creative ideas and that now is the time to act on them. The Page of Wands reminds you that your potential is limitless, and it is up to you to harness it and bring your ideas to life.

NUMEROLOGICAL SIGNIFICANCE

The Page is associated with the energy of the number eleven, representing new beginnings, initiative, and the spark of creation. The Page of Wands, as the first card in the court of Wands, embodies these qualities and emphasizes the importance of creative expression and the excitement of new ventures.

New beginnings: The energy of the Page signifies new beginnings and the start of creative projects. The Page of Wands encourages you to embrace new opportunities and to approach them with enthusiasm and confidence.

Initiative: The Page also represents initiative and the drive to take the first step. The Page of Wands reminds you to be proactive in your creative endeavors and to take the initiative to bring your ideas to life.

Spark of creation: The Page highlights the spark of creation and the potential for new ideas. The Page of Wands encourages you to tap into your creative potential and explore the possibilities that come with it.

The Page of Wands is a card of creative expression, newness, and youthful enthusiasm. It encourages you to embrace your creativity and explore new opportunities with curiosity and excitement. This card serves as a reminder that you are on the brink of a new creative journey and that your potential is limitless. Embrace the energy of "Creative expression" and trust in your ability to bring your ideas to life with enthusiasm and passion.

PAGE OF WANDS REVERSED

Lack of direction: Enthusiasm without a clear goal leads to confusion and stagnation. Define your objectives and create a plan to achieve them.

Impatience: Desire for quick results can lead to rash actions and mistakes. Practice patience and understand that growth takes time.

Missed opportunities: Distraction and lack of focus can cause you to overlook potential. Stay attentive and seize opportunities when they arise.

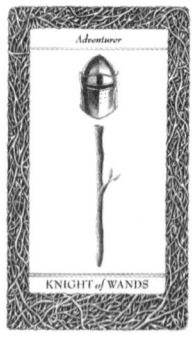

Knight *of* Wands

MEANING IN A TAROT READING

When the Knight of Wands appears in a reading, it signifies adventure, boldness, and the drive to take action. This card embodies the energy of enthusiasm, courage, and a quest for new experiences. It encourages you to embrace your inner adventurer and to pursue your goals with passion and determination.

Adventurer: The mantra of this card, "Adventurer," highlights the importance of seeking out new experiences and embracing the unknown. It suggests that you are ready to embark on a new journey and that it is time to take bold steps toward your aspirations. This card is about being fearless and open to the excitement of exploration.

Bold action: The Knight of Wands represents bold action and the willingness to take risks. It encourages you to pursue your goals with vigor and to act decisively. This card is about harnessing your courage and charging forward with confidence.

Passion and enthusiasm: This card signifies passion and enthusiasm in all your endeavors. It suggests that your energy and zest for life are driving forces that propel you toward success. The Knight of Wands reminds you to infuse your actions with passion and to stay motivated by your excitement.

Pursuit of goals: The Knight of Wands emphasizes the importance of pursuing your goals with determination and focus. It encourages you to stay committed to your path and to keep pushing forward despite any obstacles. This card is about maintaining momentum and striving for achievement.

Exploration and discovery: This card also highlights the themes of exploration and discovery. It suggests that you are on a quest to discover new opportunities and to broaden your horizons. The Knight of Wands reminds you to stay curious and to be open to the adventures that lie ahead.

NUMEROLOGICAL SIGNIFICANCE

The Knight is associated with the energy of the number twelve, representing balance, duality, and dynamic interaction. The Knight of Wands, as the second card in the court of Wands, embodies these qualities and emphasizes the importance of adventure, action, and the pursuit of new experiences.

Balance: The energy of the Knight signifies the need for balance between bold action and thoughtful consideration. The Knight of Wands encourages you to be adventurous while also staying grounded and mindful of your actions.

Duality: The Knight also represents duality and the interplay of different forces. The Knight of Wands reminds you to balance your enthusiasm with patience and to navigate the dynamic interactions in your life with grace.

Dynamic interaction: The Knight highlights the dynamic nature of action and adventure. The Knight of Wands encourages you to engage with the world around you and to embrace the excitement of new experiences and challenges.

The Knight of Wands is a card of adventure, action, and dynamic energy. It encourages you to pursue new experiences with enthusiasm and confidence while maintaining a balance between boldness and mindfulness. This card serves as a reminder to embrace life's adventures and to navigate the complexities of your journey with grace and excitement.

KNIGHT OF WANDS REVERSED

Impulsiveness: Acting without thinking through the consequences can lead to setbacks. Consider the long-term impact of your actions.

Inconsistency: Frequent changes in direction and goals can hinder progress. Commit to a course of action and follow through.

Burnout: Intense but short-lived enthusiasm can result in exhaustion. Pace yourself to maintain energy and avoid burnout.

Queen *of* Wands

MEANING IN A TAROT READING

When the Queen of Wands appears in a reading, it signifies a vibrant, charismatic, and energetic presence. This card embodies the energy of confidence, passion, and a deep "lust for life." It encourages you to embrace your dynamic spirit and to radiate warmth, enthusiasm, and vitality in all your endeavors.

Lust for life: The mantra of this card, "Lust for life," highlights the importance of embracing life with passion and enthusiasm. It suggests that you have a zest for life that inspires and energizes those around you. This card is about living life to the fullest and enjoying every moment.

Confidence and charisma: The Queen of Wands represents confidence and charisma. It encourages you to step into your power and to shine brightly. This card is about exuding self-assurance and using your magnetic personality to influence and inspire others.

Passion and creativity: This card signifies a strong connection to passion and creativity. It suggests that you are driven by your desires and that your creative energy is a powerful force in your life. The Queen of Wands reminds you to channel your passion into your projects and relationships.

Warmth and generosity: The Queen of Wands emphasizes the importance of warmth and generosity. It encourages you to be openhearted and to share your energy and enthusiasm with others. This card is about being supportive and uplifting, creating a positive and nurturing environment.

Determination and leadership: This card also highlights the themes of determination and leadership. It suggests that you have the strength and resolve to achieve your goals and to lead others with confidence and grace. The Queen of Wands reminds you to stay focused and to use your leadership abilities to guide and inspire.

NUMEROLOGICAL SIGNIFICANCE

In numerology, the Queen is associated with the energy of the number thirteen, representing creativity, communication, and growth. The Queen of Wands, as the third card in the court of Wands, embodies these qualities and emphasizes the importance of passion, creativity, and a vibrant lust for life.

Creativity: The energy of the Queen signifies creativity and the ability to bring new ideas to life. The Queen of Wands encourages you to embrace your creative potential and to use it to enhance your experiences and relationships.

Communication: The Queen also represents communication and the power of expression. The Queen of Wands reminds you to share your thoughts and ideas with confidence and to use your voice to inspire and motivate others.

Growth: The Queen highlights the importance of personal and collective growth. The Queen of Wands encourages you to pursue your passions and to foster an environment that supports and nurtures growth and development.

The Queen of Wands is a card of vibrant energy, confidence, and a deep lust for life. It encourages you to embrace your dynamic spirit and to radiate warmth, enthusiasm, and vitality in all that you do. This card serves as a reminder that you have the power to inspire and uplift others, and that your passion and creativity are powerful forces in your life. Embrace the energy of "Lust for life" and trust in your ability to live life to the fullest with confidence and joy.

QUEEN OF WANDS REVERSED

Envy: Envying others' success can create resentment. Focus on your own path and celebrate others' achievements without comparison.

Domineering: Overbearing behavior can strain relationships. Practice empathy and respect others' autonomy.

Lack of confidence: Self-doubt can hold you back from reaching your full potential. Build confidence through positive self-talk and celebrating small wins.

King *of* Wands

MEANING IN A TAROT READING

When the King of Wands appears in a reading, it signifies dynamic leadership, vision, and the ability to inspire others. This card embodies the energy of "creative leadership," where innovation and authority blend to guide and motivate those around you. It encourages you to embrace your leadership qualities and lead confidently, creatively, and passionately.

Creative leadership: The mantra of this card, "Creative leadership," highlights the importance of leading with vision and innovation. It suggests that you can inspire and guide others through your creative ideas and dynamic presence. This card is about using your leadership skills to foster creativity and progress.

Visionary thinking: The King of Wands represents visionary thinking and the ability to see the bigger picture. It encourages you to set ambitious goals and to lead others toward achieving them. This card is about having a clear vision and the determination to turn it into reality.

Confidence and authority: This card signifies confidence and authority in leadership. It suggests that you possess the self-assurance and strength needed to lead effectively. The King of Wands reminds you to trust in your abilities and to lead with conviction and integrity.

Inspiration and motivation: The King of Wands emphasizes the importance of inspiring and motivating others. It encourages you to use your enthusiasm and passion to uplift those around you. This card is about being a role model and empowering others to reach their full potential.

Dynamic action: This card also highlights the themes of dynamic action and decisive leadership. It suggests that you can take bold steps and make swift decisions. The King of Wands reminds you to act with confidence and to lead with a sense of purpose and direction.

NUMEROLOGICAL SIGNIFICANCE

The King is associated with the energy of the number fourteen, representing stability, structure, and authority. The King of Wands, as the fourteenth card in the court of Wands, embodies these qualities and emphasizes the importance of creative leadership and the ability to inspire and guide others.

Stability: The energy of the King signifies stability and the ability to create a strong foundation. The King of Wands encourages you to build a stable and supportive environment where creativity and innovation can flourish.

Structure: The King also represents structure and the importance of organization in leadership. The King of Wands reminds you to use your organizational skills to manage your projects and to lead others effectively.

Authority: The King highlights the importance of authority and the ability to lead with confidence. The King of Wands encourages you to embrace your leadership role and to use your authority to guide and inspire others.

The King of Wands is a card of dynamic leadership, vision, and the ability to inspire and motivate others. It encourages you to embrace your role as a creative leader and to lead with confidence, creativity, and passion. This card serves as a reminder that you have the power to guide others toward success and to create a supportive and innovative environment. Embrace the energy of "Creative leadership" and trust in your ability to lead with vision and integrity.

KING OF WANDS REVERSED

Tyranny: Using power irresponsibly can create conflict. Lead with integrity and fairness.

Impulsivity: Hasty decisions without considering consequences can cause problems. Take time to think things through before acting.

Unfocused vision: Scattered energy and lack of clear goals can hinder progress. Clarify your vision and create a road map to achieve it.

THE SUIT OF CUPS

Ace *of* Cups

MEANING IN A TAROT READING

When the Ace of Cups appears in a reading, it signifies new beginnings in matters of the heart, emotional fulfillment, and the overflowing of love and compassion. This card embodies the energy of "a new start for the heart," highlighting the potential for profound emotional renewal and the beginning of a joyful and loving phase in your life. It encourages you to open your heart to new experiences and embrace the love and emotional growth that comes your way.

A new start for the heart: This card's mantra, "A new start for the heart," emphasizes the importance of embracing new emotional beginnings. It suggests that you are on the brink of experiencing profound emotional renewal and the start of a loving, fulfilling phase in your life.

Emotional fulfillment: The Ace of Cups represents the overflowing of emotions and the abundance of love. It encourages you to embrace your feelings fully and to allow yourself to experience joy, love, and compassion without reservation.

New relationships: This card often signifies the beginning of new relationships, whether romantic, platonic, or familial. New connections will bring emotional fulfillment and joy into your life. Be open to forming deep and meaningful bonds with others.

Healing and renewal: The Ace of Cups highlights the themes of healing and emotional renewal. It encourages you to let go of past emotional wounds and to embrace the healing process. This is a time for emotional cleansing and starting anew with a fresh perspective.

Spiritual awakening: This card also signifies a spiritual awakening and a deepening of your connection to the divine. It encourages you to explore your spiritual path and to allow your heart to guide you toward greater understanding and enlightenment.

NUMEROLOGICAL SIGNIFICANCE

The Ace is associated with the energy of the number one, representing new beginnings, potential, and the start of a new cycle. The Ace of Cups, as the first card in the suit of Cups, embodies these qualities and emphasizes the importance of emotional renewal and the beginning of a joyful phase in your life.

New beginnings: The energy of the Ace signifies new beginnings and the start of a new emotional cycle. The Ace of Cups encourages you to embrace new opportunities for love and emotional growth.

Potential: The Ace also represents potential and the promise of new experiences. The Ace of Cups reminds you that your heart is open to receiving and giving love and that new emotional experiences are on the horizon.

The start of a new cycle: The Ace highlights the start of a new cycle in your emotional and spiritual journey. The Ace of Cups encourages you to embrace this new phase with an open heart and a positive attitude.

The Ace of Cups is a card of new beginnings, emotional fulfillment, and the overflowing of love and compassion. It encourages you to embrace "a new start for the heart" and to open yourself to new emotional experiences and connections. This card serves as a reminder that you are on the brink of a joyful and loving phase in your life and that your heart is ready to receive and give love. Embrace the energy of emotional renewal and allow your heart to guide you toward deeper connections and greater fulfillment.

ACE OF CUPS REVERSED

Emotional block: Difficulty expressing or understanding emotions can lead to isolation. Work on emotional intelligence and communication.

Missed connections: Relationships may not be deepening as hoped, causing disappointment. Invest time and effort into meaningful connections.

Disappointment: Unmet emotional needs lead to feelings of unfulfillment. Identify your emotional needs and seek ways to fulfill them.

Two *of* Cups

MEANING IN A TAROT READING

When the Two of Cups appears in a reading, it signifies harmonious partnerships, mutual understanding, and the deepening of emotional connections. This card embodies the energy of "on the same page," highlighting the importance of mutual respect, shared goals, and emotional harmony in relationships. It encourages you to embrace the bonds you share with others and to nurture the connections that bring balance and joy into your life.

On the same page: The mantra of this card, "On the same page," emphasizes the importance of mutual understanding and harmony in relationships. It suggests that you and someone else are in sync, sharing similar values, goals, and emotions.

Harmonious partnerships: The Two of Cups represents harmonious partnerships and the blending of energies between two people. It encourages you to nurture the relationships that bring balance and joy into your life, whether they are romantic, platonic, or professional.

Mutual understanding: This card signifies mutual understanding and respect. It suggests that you and another person see eye to eye and that your connection is built on a foundation of trust and shared values.

Emotional bonding: The Two of Cups highlights the deepening of emotional bonds. It encourages you to open your heart and to embrace the emotional connections that enrich your life. This is a time to celebrate the love and support you receive from others.

Reconciliation: This card can also indicate reconciliation and the healing of past rifts. Any misunderstandings or conflicts can be resolved through open communication and mutual understanding.

NUMEROLOGICAL SIGNIFICANCE

In numerology, the number two represents balance, duality, and partnership. The Two of Cups, as the second card in the suit of Cups, embodies these qualities and emphasizes the importance of harmonious relationships and mutual understanding.

Balance: The energy of the Two signifies balance and the importance of finding harmony in your relationships. The Two of Cups encourages you to create a balanced and supportive connection with others.

Duality: The Two also represents duality and the interplay of two energies coming together. The Two of Cups reminds you that partnerships are about give and take and that mutual respect and understanding are key.

Partnership: The Two highlights the importance of partnership and the value of working together toward shared goals. The Two of Cups encourages you to celebrate the partnerships in your life and to nurture the connections that bring you joy.

The Two of Cups is a card of harmonious partnerships, mutual understanding, and emotional bonding. It encourages you to embrace the energy of being "on the same page" and to nurture the relationships that bring balance and joy into your life. This card serves as a reminder that mutual respect, shared goals, and emotional harmony are the foundations of strong and fulfilling connections. Embrace the love and support you receive from others, and celebrate the deepening of your emotional bonds.

TWO OF CUPS REVERSED

Disharmony: Conflicts or misunderstandings in relationships cause tension. Open communication and empathy are key to resolving issues.

Breakups: Potential separation or loss of connection, leading to emotional pain. Allow yourself to grieve and heal.

Imbalance: Unequal give and take in relationships creates frustration. Strive for balance and mutual support.

Three *of* Cups

MEANING IN A TAROT READING

When the Three of Cups appears in a reading, it signifies celebration, joy, and the importance of community and friendship. This card embodies the energy of "joy," highlighting moments of happiness, shared experiences, and the uplifting power of coming together with others. It encourages you to embrace life's joyous moments and celebrate with those who support and uplift you.

Joy: The mantra of this card, "Joy," emphasizes the importance of celebrating the happy moments in life. It suggests that you are in a phase where joy and happiness are abundant, and it encourages you to share these moments with others.

Celebration: The Three of Cups represents celebration and the joy that comes from gathering with friends and loved ones. It encourages you to take time to celebrate your achievements, milestones, and the positive aspects of your life.

Community and friendship: This card highlights the importance of community and friendship. It suggests that your relationships with others are a source of joy and support, and it encourages you to nurture these connections.

Shared experiences: The Three of Cups signifies the joy that comes from shared experiences and collaboration. It encourages you to engage in activities that bring people together and to celebrate the collective achievements of your community.

Emotional support: This card also represents the emotional support and encouragement you receive from those around you. It reminds you to appreciate the people who stand by you and to celebrate the bonds that bring joy into your life.

NUMEROLOGICAL SIGNIFICANCE

In numerology, the number three represents creativity, expression, and growth. The Three of Cups, as the third card in the suit of Cups, embodies these qualities and emphasizes the importance of joy, celebration, and community.

Creativity: The energy of the Three signifies creativity and the joy that comes from creative expression. The Three of Cups encourages you to engage in activities that bring out your creative side and to share these experiences with others.

Expression: The Three also represents expression and the importance of expressing your emotions and celebrating openly. The Three of Cups reminds you that sharing your joy with others enhances the experience and strengthens your bonds.

Growth: The Three highlights the importance of growth and the positive outcomes that come from collaboration and shared experiences. The Three of Cups encourages you to embrace the growth that results from being part of a supportive community.

The Three of Cups is a card of celebration, joy, and the importance of community and friendship. It encourages you to embrace the energy of "joy" and to celebrate the happy moments in your life with those who support and uplift you. This card serves as a reminder that joy is multiplied when shared and that your relationships and community are sources of happiness and fulfillment.

Embrace the celebrations, nurture your connections, and find joy in the shared experiences that bring you closer to others.

THREE OF CUPS REVERSED

Isolation: Feeling left out or excluded from social groups can cause loneliness. Seek out new social connections and engage in community activities.

Overindulgence: Excessive partying or superficial relationships lead to emptiness. Focus on meaningful interactions and moderation.

Gossip: Negative talk affecting friendships and trust, causing conflict. Avoid gossip and foster honest communication.

Four *of* Cups

MEANING IN A TAROT READING

When the Four of Cups appears in a reading, it signifies a period of introspection, discontent, and potential stagnation. This card embodies the energy of "Snap out of it," highlighting the importance of breaking free from apathy, reevaluating your situation, and recognizing the opportunities that are being offered to you. It encourages you to shift your focus from what is lacking to what is possible and to reengage with the world around you.

Snap out of it: This card's mantra, "Snap out of it," emphasizes the need to awaken from a state of discontent or indifference. It suggests that you are missing opportunities due to focusing on what is missing or dissatisfaction with your current situation.

Introspection: The Four of Cups represents a period of introspection and self-reflection. It encourages you to look within and to understand the root of your discontent. It may be a time to reevaluate your desires and motivations.

Discontent: This card signifies feelings of discontent and dissatisfaction. It suggests that you may feel emotionally unfulfilled or disconnected from your surroundings. Recognize these feelings and seek ways to address them.

Missed opportunities: The Four of Cups highlights the potential for missed opportunities. It reminds you to stay open and aware of the possibilities around you. Avoid letting apathy or discontent prevent you from seeing what is being offered.

Reengagement: This card encourages reengagement with life and the world around you. By shifting your focus and perspective, you can rediscover a sense of purpose and fulfillment.

NUMEROLOGICAL SIGNIFICANCE

In numerology, the number four represents stability, structure, and foundation. The Four of Cups, as the fourth card in the suit of Cups, embodies these qualities and emphasizes the need for emotional stability and the importance of being open to opportunities.

Stability: The energy of the Four signifies the need for stability and grounding in your emotional life. The Four of Cups encourages you to find a stable foundation from which to address your feelings of discontent.

Structure: The Four also represents structure and the importance of creating a supportive framework for your emotional well-being. The Four of Cups reminds you to build a structure that supports your emotional needs and helps you stay open to new possibilities.

Foundation: The Four highlights the importance of establishing a strong emotional foundation. The Four of Cups encourages you to address any underlying issues causing your discontent, and to build a foundation that allows for emotional growth and fulfillment.

The Four of Cups is a card of introspection, discontent, and the need to break free from apathy. It encourages you to embrace the energy of "Snap out of it" and to reengage with life by recognizing the opportunities that are available to you. This card serves as a reminder that while periods of introspection are valuable, it is also important to stay open and aware of the possibilities around you. Shift your focus from what is lacking to what is possible, and to reengage with the world to find emotional fulfillment and purpose.

FOUR OF CUPS REVERSED

Awakening: Realizing missed opportunities, renewing interest and enthusiasm. Embrace new possibilities with an open heart.

Moving forward: Letting go of apathy and taking action to improve your situation. Be proactive in pursuing your goals.

New perspectives: Gaining a fresh outlook on life, seeing possibilities and potential. Open your mind to new ideas and experiences.

Five *of* Cups

MEANING IN A TAROT READING

When the Five of Cups appears in a reading, it signifies loss, disappointment, and a focus on what has gone wrong rather than what remains. This card embodies the energy of "Turn around," highlighting the importance of shifting your perspective from what is lost to what is still available. It encourages you to acknowledge your grief but also to recognize the potential for healing and new opportunities that await once you change your focus.

Turn around: The mantra of this card, "Turn around," emphasizes the need to shift your perspective from loss to potential. It suggests that while it is important to acknowledge your grief, you should also be open to seeing what remains and what new possibilities lie ahead.

Acknowledging loss: The Five of Cups represents a period of mourning and disappointment. It encourages you to experience and process your loss and sorrow fully. It is a necessary step in the healing process.

Disappointment: This card signifies feelings of disappointment and regret. It suggests that you may be dwelling on what went wrong and feeling stuck in negative emotions. Recognize these feelings and allow yourself to grieve.

Shift in focus: The Five of Cups highlights the importance of shifting your focus from what is lost to what is still available. It reminds you that there are still opportunities and positive aspects in your life that you may be overlooking.

Healing and moving forward: This card encourages healing and moving forward. By changing your perspective and focusing on the positive, you can begin to heal and open yourself up to new possibilities and opportunities.

NUMEROLOGICAL SIGNIFICANCE

In numerology, the number five represents change, challenge, and growth. The Five of Cups, as the fifth card in the suit of Cups, embodies these qualities and emphasizes the need for adaptability and resilience in the face of emotional challenges.

Change: The energy of the Five signifies change and the importance of adapting to new circumstances. The Five of Cups encourages you to embrace change as a part of life and to see it as an opportunity for growth.

Challenge: The Five also represents a challenge and the need to overcome obstacles. The Five of Cups reminds you that while emotional challenges can be difficult, they are also opportunities for personal growth and transformation.

Growth: The Five highlights the importance of growth through adversity. The Five of Cups encourages you to learn from your experiences and to use them as a catalyst for emotional and spiritual growth.

The Five of Cups is a card of loss, disappointment, and the need to shift your perspective. It encourages you to embrace the energy of "Turn around" and to focus on what remains rather than what is lost. This card serves as a reminder that while it is important to acknowledge your grief and disappointment, it is equally important to recognize the potential for healing and new opportunities. By changing your focus and being open to the positive aspects of your life, you can begin to heal and move forward with renewed hope and resilience.

FIVE OF CUPS REVERSED

Healing: Recovering from grief, finding acceptance and peace. Allow yourself to heal and move forward.

Forgiveness: Letting go of past hurts, mending relationships and moving on. Practice forgiveness for yourself and others.

Renewed hope: Seeing positive possibilities again, finding optimism and joy. Focus on the positive aspects of life.

Six *of* Cups

MEANING IN A TAROT READING

When the Six of Cups appears in a reading, it signifies nostalgia, childhood memories, and the warmth of past experiences. This card embodies the energy of "nostalgia," highlighting the importance of reconnecting with your past, cherishing fond memories, and finding joy in simple, heartfelt moments. It encourages you to reflect on your history and to allow your past's positive aspects to influence your present and future.

Nostalgia: The mantra of this card, "Nostalgia," emphasizes the importance of reconnecting with your past. The card suggests that revisiting happy memories and childhood experiences can bring comfort, joy, and a sense of grounding.

Childhood memories: The Six of Cups represents the innocence and joy of childhood. It encourages you to reconnect with the carefree, playful aspects of your past and to find happiness in simple pleasures.

Reunion and reconnection: This card signifies reunion and reconnection with people from your past. It suggests that reconnecting with old friends or family members can bring a sense of fulfillment and joy.

Emotional healing: The Six of Cups highlights the healing power of positive memories. It encourages you to draw on the warmth and love of your past to heal current emotional wounds and to foster a sense of inner peace.

Generosity and kindness: This card also represents acts of kindness and generosity. Giving and receiving kindness, especially with those from your past, can create a positive ripple effect in your life.

NUMEROLOGICAL SIGNIFICANCE

In numerology, the number six represents harmony, balance, and nurturing. The Six of Cups, as the sixth card in the suit of Cups, embodies these qualities and emphasizes the importance of finding emotional balance and harmony through reconnecting with your past.

Harmony: The energy of the Six signifies harmony and the importance of creating balance in your emotional life. The Six of Cups encourages you to find peace and joy by reconnecting with positive memories and experiences.

Balance: The Six also represents balance and the need to integrate your past with your present. The Six of Cups reminds you that your past experiences can provide valuable lessons and insights that help you navigate your current situation.

Nurturing: The Six highlights the importance of nurturing your emotional well-being. The Six of Cups encourages you to care for your inner child and to seek comfort and joy in the positive aspects of your past.

The Six of Cups is a card of nostalgia, childhood memories, and the warmth of past experiences. It encourages you to embrace the energy of "nostalgia" and to reconnect with the positive aspects of your past. This card serves as a reminder that revisiting happy memories and reconnecting with people from your past can bring comfort, joy, and a sense of grounding. By cherishing these moments and allowing them to influence your present, you can find emotional balance and harmony. Celebrate the simple, heartfelt joys of life and let the warmth of your past light your way forward.

SIX OF CUPS REVERSED

Stuck in the past: Unable to move on from past memories, causing stagnation. Focus on the present and future.

Nostalgia: Overly idealizing the past, ignoring the present and future. Balance fond memories with current realities.

Unresolved issues: Past conflicts resurfacing, needing closure and resolution. Address unresolved issues to find peace.

Seven *of* Cups

MEANING IN A TAROT READING

When the Seven of Cups appears in a reading, it signifies choices, illusions, and the allure of possibilities. This card embodies the energy of "Not everything that glitters is gold," highlighting the importance of discernment and caution when faced with multiple options. It encourages you to look beyond surface appearances and evaluate your choices carefully to avoid illusions and false promises.

Not everything that glitters is gold: The mantra of this card, "Not everything that glitters is gold," emphasizes the need for discernment and caution. While many opportunities may seem attractive, not all are as valuable or beneficial as they appear.

Choices and options: The Seven of Cups represents a plethora of choices and possibilities. It encourages you to explore your options but also to be mindful of the potential illusions and distractions that may come with them.

Illusions and fantasies: This card signifies the presence of illusions and fantasies. This card suggests that you may be tempted by unrealistic or overly idealistic visions. Be wary of chasing after dreams that may not be grounded in reality.

Discernment and caution: The Seven of Cups highlights the importance of discernment and caution when making decisions. It encourages you to look beyond surface appearances and to evaluate the true value and potential of each option carefully.

Decision-making: This card also represents the challenge of making decisions amid a multitude of choices. Taking time to reflect and consider your options will lead to better outcomes than making impulsive decisions.

NUMEROLOGICAL SIGNIFICANCE

In numerology, the number seven represents introspection, analysis, and spiritual insight. The Seven of Cups, as the seventh card in the suit of Cups, embodies these qualities and emphasizes the need for careful consideration and inner reflection when faced with multiple choices.

Introspection: The energy of the Seven signifies introspection and the importance of looking within to understand your true desires and motivations. The Seven of Cups encourages you to take time for self-reflection before making decisions.

Analysis: The Seven also represents analysis and the need for careful evaluation of your options. The Seven of Cups reminds you to weigh the pros and cons of each choice and to seek clarity before moving forward.

Spiritual insight: The Seven highlights the importance of spiritual insight and intuition. The Seven of Cups encourages you to trust your inner wisdom and to seek guidance from your higher self when faced with complex decisions.

The Seven of Cups is a card of choices, illusions, and the allure of possibilities. It encourages you to embrace the energy of "Not everything that glitters is gold" and to approach your options with discernment and caution. This card serves as a reminder that while many opportunities may seem attractive, it is essential to look beyond surface appearances and to evaluate the true value and potential of each choice carefully. By taking time for introspection and analysis, you can avoid illusions and make decisions that are aligned with your true desires and goals. Trust your inner wisdom and seek clarity to navigate through the myriads of possibilities.

SEVEN OF CUPS REVERSED

Clarity: Seeing through illusions, making informed and realistic choices. Focus on practical solutions and achievable goals.

Focus: Concentrating on realistic goals, cutting through distractions and fantasies. Stay grounded and prioritize tasks.

Decisiveness: Making clear decisions, no longer overwhelmed by options and possibilities. Trust your judgment and take action.

Eight *of* Cups

MEANING IN A TAROT READING

When the Eight of Cups appears in a reading, it signifies a decision to leave behind something that is no longer fulfilling or meaningful. This card embodies the energy of "the right to walk away," highlighting the importance of recognizing when it is time to move on and pursue a more fulfilling path. It encourages you to honor your emotional needs and to have the courage to leave situations that no longer serve your highest good.

The right to walk away: The mantra of this card, "The right to walk away," emphasizes the importance of recognizing when it is time to let go. It suggests that you have the right to leave behind situations, relationships, or endeavors that are no longer fulfilling.

Seeking fulfillment: The Eight of Cups represents the search for deeper meaning and emotional fulfillment. It encourages you to pursue what truly brings you joy and satisfaction, even if it means leaving behind what is familiar or comfortable.

Letting go: This card signifies the act of letting go and moving on from the past. It suggests that holding on to what no longer serves you can prevent you from finding true happiness and fulfillment.

Emotional courage: The Eight of Cups highlights the need for emotional courage to walk away from unfulfilling situations. It encourages you to trust your instincts and to prioritize your emotional well-being.

Personal growth: This card also represents personal growth and the journey toward self-discovery. It suggests that by leaving behind what no longer serves you, you open yourself up to new opportunities for growth and fulfillment.

NUMEROLOGICAL SIGNIFICANCE

In numerology, the number eight represents power, strength, and transformation. The Eight of Cups, as the eighth card in the suit of Cups, embodies these qualities and emphasizes the importance of using your inner strength to make transformative decisions.

Power: The energy of the Eight signifies personal power and the ability to take control of your life. The Eight of Cups encourages you to empower yourself by making decisions that align with your true desires and values.

Strength: The Eight also represents inner strength and the courage to face difficult decisions. The Eight of Cups reminds you that you have the strength to walk away from what no longer serves you, and to pursue a more fulfilling path.

Transformation: The Eight highlights the importance of transformation and the potential for growth through change. The Eight of Cups encourages you to embrace the transformative power of letting go and to seek new opportunities for personal and emotional growth.

The Eight of Cups is a card of leaving behind, seeking fulfillment, and emotional courage. It encourages you to embrace the energy of "the right to walk away" and to recognize when it is time to move on from situations, relationships, or endeavors that no longer serve your highest good. This card serves as a reminder that you have the power and strength to make transformative decisions that lead to greater emotional fulfillment and personal growth. Trust your instincts, honor your emotional needs, and have the courage to pursue a more meaningful and satisfying path.

EIGHT OF CUPS REVERSED

Stagnation: Fear of moving on, staying in unfulfilling situations out of comfort. Embrace change and seek growth.

Returning: Going back to a situation previously left, reconsidering past decisions. Reflect on past choices and their impact.

Emotional clinginess: Difficulty letting go emotionally, holding on to the past. Practice emotional release and healing.

Nine *of* Cups

MEANING IN A TAROT READING
When the Nine of Cups appears in a reading, it signifies contentment, satisfaction, and the fulfillment of desires. This card embodies the energy of "Enjoy this moment," highlighting the importance of appreciating the present and celebrating your achievements. It encourages you to embrace the joy and abundance in your life and to take a moment to savor your successes and the happiness they bring.

Enjoy this moment: The mantra of this card, "Enjoy this moment," emphasizes the importance of being present and appreciating the joy and fulfillment in your life. It suggests that you take time to savor the happiness and contentment you have achieved.

Contentment: The Nine of Cups represents a state of contentment and emotional satisfaction. It encourages you to recognize and appreciate the blessings in your life and to feel grateful for what you have accomplished.

Fulfillment of desires: This card signifies the fulfillment of wishes and desires. It suggests that your efforts have paid off and that you are experiencing the rewards of your hard work and determination.

Gratitude: The Nine of Cups highlights the importance of gratitude. It encourages you to acknowledge the positive aspects of your life and to express gratitude for the abundance and joy you are experiencing.

Celebration: This card also represents celebration and the enjoyment of life's pleasures. It suggests that you take time to celebrate your achievements and to share your happiness with others.

NUMEROLOGICAL SIGNIFICANCE
In numerology, the number nine represents completion, fulfillment, and wisdom. The Nine of Cups, as the ninth card in the suit of Cups, embodies these qualities and emphasizes the importance of appreciating the completion of a cycle and the fulfillment it brings.

Completion: The energy of the Nine signifies the completion of a cycle and the achievement of goals. The Nine of Cups encourages you to recognize and celebrate the culmination of your efforts and the satisfaction it brings.

Fulfillment: The Nine also represents fulfillment and the attainment of desires. The Nine of Cups reminds you to appreciate the fulfillment of your wishes and to feel content with your achievements.

Wisdom: The Nine highlights the importance of wisdom gained through experience. The Nine of Cups encourages you to reflect on the journey that brought you to this point and to appreciate the lessons learned along the way.

The Nine of Cups is a card of contentment, satisfaction, and the fulfillment of desires. It encourages you to embrace the energy of "Enjoy this moment" and to appreciate the joy and abundance in your life. This card serves as a reminder to be present, to savor your successes, and to feel grateful for the blessings you have received. Celebrate your achievements, express gratitude, and take time to enjoy the happiness and fulfillment that comes from the completion of a cycle. By appreciating the present moment, you can fully experience life's joy and contentment.

NINE OF CUPS REVERSED

Dissatisfaction: Unmet desires, feeling unfulfilled despite success and achievements. Reevaluate what truly brings you happiness.

Overindulgence: Excessive pleasure seeking, leading to negative outcomes and emptiness. Practice moderation and self-control.

False contentment: Superficial happiness, ignoring deeper needs and desires. Seek meaningful fulfillment beyond material success.

Ten *of* Cups

MEANING IN A TAROT READING

When the Ten of Cups appears in a reading, it signifies ultimate happiness, emotional fulfillment, and harmonious relationships. This card embodies the energy of "wishes fulfilled," highlighting the realization of dreams and the attainment of deep emotional contentment. It encourages you to cherish the joy and harmony in your life and to celebrate the love and unity you share with those around you.

Wishes fulfilled: The mantra of this card, "Wishes fulfilled," emphasizes the culmination of your desires and the deep sense of satisfaction that comes from achieving your dreams. It suggests that you are experiencing a time of great joy and emotional abundance.

Ultimate happiness: The Ten of Cups represents a state of ultimate happiness and emotional fulfillment. It encourages you to recognize and appreciate your profound joy and contentment.

Harmonious relationships: This card signifies harmonious relationships and the strong bonds of love and unity within your family and community. Your connections with others are a source of great joy and support.

Emotional fulfillment: The Ten of Cups highlights the attainment of deep emotional fulfillment. It encourages you to cherish the emotional richness in your life and to continue nurturing the relationships that bring you happiness.

Celebration of love: This card also represents the celebration of love and the joy of sharing your life with loved ones. It suggests that you take time to celebrate the love and unity in your relationships.

NUMEROLOGICAL SIGNIFICANCE

In numerology, the number ten represents completion, wholeness, and the beginning of a new cycle. The Ten of Cups, as the tenth card in the suit of Cups, embodies these qualities and emphasizes the importance of celebrating the completion of a journey and the fulfillment it brings.

Completion: The energy of the Ten signifies the completion of a journey and the achievement of your goals. The Ten of Cups encourages you to recognize and celebrate the culmination of your efforts and the profound sense of fulfillment it brings.

Wholeness: The Ten also represents wholeness and the attainment of a state of completeness. The Ten of Cups reminds you to appreciate the sense of wholeness and emotional abundance in your life.

New cycle: The Ten highlights the beginning of a new cycle, suggesting that the fulfillment you are experiencing is the foundation for future growth and happiness.

The Ten of Cups encourages you to embrace this new phase with joy and optimism.

The Ten of Cups is a card of ultimate happiness, emotional fulfillment, and harmonious relationships. It encourages you to embrace the energy of "Wishes fulfilled" and to celebrate the realization of your dreams and the deep sense of satisfaction it brings. This card serves as a reminder to cherish the joy and harmony in your life, nurture your relationships, and appreciate the profound emotional fulfillment you have achieved. Celebrate the love and unity in your life and recognize the completion of a journey that has brought you to a place of great joy and contentment.

TEN OF CUPS REVERSED
Family conflict: Disruptions or discord in the family unit, causing tension and sadness. Address conflicts with empathy and understanding.

Unrealistic expectations: Idealizing relationships, leading to disappointment and frustration. Set realistic expectations and communicate openly.

Broken dreams: Hopes for happiness not realized, feeling let down and disheartened. Focus on rebuilding and finding new paths to joy.

Page *of* Cups

MEANING IN A TAROT READING

When the Page of Cups appears in a reading, it signifies new beginnings in emotional and creative realms, embodying a sense of youthful curiosity and openness. This card embodies the energy of "Open yourself to love," highlighting the importance of embracing new emotional experiences and being vulnerable. It encourages you to approach life with a sense of wonder and to be open to the love and creativity that the universe offers.

Open yourself to love: The mantra of this card, "Open yourself to love," emphasizes the importance of being open and receptive to new emotional experiences. It suggests that you allow your heart to be vulnerable and embrace the possibilities of love and deep connections.

New emotional beginnings: The Page of Cups represents new beginnings in the realm of emotions. It encourages you to explore your feelings and to be open to the new and unexpected in your emotional life.

Youthful curiosity: This card signifies a sense of youthful curiosity and wonder. It suggests that you approach life with an open heart and a willingness to explore new emotional and creative experiences.

Creativity and inspiration: The Page of Cups highlights the importance of creativity and inspiration. It encourages you to express yourself creatively and to allow your emotions to inspire your creative endeavors.

Emotional vulnerability: This card also represents emotional vulnerability and the courage to be open and honest with your feelings. By being vulnerable, you can form deeper and more-meaningful connections with others.

NUMEROLOGICAL SIGNIFICANCE

The number eleven associated with the Page represents beginnings, potential, and a youthful approach. The Page of Cups embodies these qualities and emphasizes the importance of openness and receptivity in emotional and creative realms.

Beginnings: The energy of the Page signifies new beginnings and the start of a new emotional or creative journey. The Page of Cups encourages you to embrace new experiences with an open heart.

Potential: The Page also represents potential and the promise of what can be. The Page of Cups reminds you that you can unlock new possibilities and opportunities by being open to love and creativity.

Youthful approach: The Page highlights the importance of a youthful approach to life. The Page of Cups encourages you to maintain a sense of curiosity and wonder and to be willing to explore new emotional and creative realms.

The Page of Cups is a card of new beginnings, youthful curiosity, and openness to emotional and creative experiences. It encourages you to embrace the energy of "Open yourself to love" and to allow your heart to be vulnerable and receptive. This card serves as a reminder to approach life with a sense of wonder, to be open to new emotional experiences, and to express yourself creatively. By being open and receptive, you can form deeper connections, unlock new possibilities, and find inspiration in the world around you. Celebrate the potential for love and creativity in your life and allow yourself to be guided by your heart.

PAGE OF CUPS REVERSED

Immaturity: Emotional naivety, struggling with understanding and expressing feelings. Work on emotional maturity and self-awareness.

Creative block: Difficulty expressing creativity, feeling uninspired and stuck. Find new sources of inspiration and explore different creative outlets.

Repressed emotions: Avoiding dealing with feelings, leading to unresolved issues. Allow yourself to process and express emotions.

Knight *of* Cups

MEANING IN A TAROT READING

When the Knight of Cups appears in a reading, it signifies romantic gestures, emotional offers, and the pursuit of dreams. This card embodies the energy of "an offer," highlighting the importance of being open to receiving and making emotional proposals. It encourages you to embrace your romantic and idealistic nature, pursue your heartfelt desires, and be ready to accept the emotional opportunities that come your way.

An offer: The mantra of this card, "An offer," emphasizes the importance of being open to giving and receiving emotional and romantic offers. It suggests that significant emotional proposals or opportunities are on the horizon.

Romantic gestures: The Knight of Cups represents romantic gestures and actions driven by emotion. It encourages you to express your feelings openly and to make heartfelt gestures to those you care about.

Pursuit of dreams: This card signifies the pursuit of dreams and ideals. It suggests that you are on a quest to achieve your emotional and creative aspirations, guided by your heart and intuition.

Emotional proposals: The Knight of Cups highlights the importance of emotional proposals and invitations. It encourages you to be receptive to offers of love, friendship, or creative collaboration and to make your own offers with sincerity and passion.

Idealism and creativity: This card also represents idealism and a creative approach to life. It suggests that you follow your heart and let your ideals and creativity guide you toward fulfilling your dreams.

NUMEROLOGICAL SIGNIFICANCE

The number twelve associated with the Knight represents action, movement, and the pursuit of goals. The Knight of Cups embodies these qualities and emphasizes the importance of taking action on emotional and creative fronts.

Action: The energy of the Knight signifies taking action and moving forward. The Knight of Cups encourages you to actively pursue your emotional and creative goals and to make meaningful gestures toward others.

Movement: The Knight also represents movement and the journey toward your dreams. The Knight of Cups reminds you to stay motivated and to keep moving toward your heartfelt desires.

Pursuit of goals: The Knight highlights the importance of pursuing your goals with passion and dedication. The Knight of Cups encourages you to follow your heart and to let your emotions and creativity drive your actions.

The Knight of Cups is a card of romantic gestures, emotional offers, and the pursuit of dreams. It encourages you to embrace the energy of "an offer" and to be open to giving and receiving emotional proposals. This card serves as a reminder to express your feelings openly, to pursue your emotional and creative aspirations with passion, and to be receptive to the opportunities that come your way. Follow your heart, make meaningful gestures, and let your ideals and creativity guide you toward fulfilling your dreams. Celebrate the journey of emotional and creative pursuit and be ready to accept and make offers that resonate with your deepest desires.

KNIGHT OF CUPS REVERSED

Moodiness: Inconsistent emotions, unpredictability and instability. Practice emotional regulation and stability.

Deception: Being misled by emotions or romantic fantasies, leading to disappointment. Ground yourself in reality and seek clarity.

Unrealistic ideals: Chasing unattainable dreams, leading to frustration and disillusionment. Set achievable goals and manage expectations.

Queen *of* Cups

MEANING IN A TAROT READING

When the Queen of Cups appears in a reading, it signifies emotional depth, compassion, and intuitive wisdom. This card embodies the energy of "heart wisdom," highlighting the importance of trusting your emotional intelligence and nurturing your inner and outer worlds with love and compassion. It encourages you to embrace your empathetic nature, to listen to your heart, and to use your intuitive insights to guide your decisions and interactions.

Heart wisdom: The mantra of this card, "Heart wisdom," emphasizes the importance of listening to and trusting your heart. Your emotional intelligence and intuitive insights are key to navigating your life with compassion and understanding.

Emotional depth: The Queen of Cups represents emotional depth and the ability to connect with your feelings on a profound level. It encourages you to explore and honor your emotions, allowing them to inform your actions and decisions.

Compassion: This card signifies compassion and the nurturing of others. It suggests that you have a natural ability to offer support and understanding to those around you, and it encourages you to continue nurturing your relationships with love and kindness.

Intuitive wisdom: The Queen of Cups highlights the importance of intuitive wisdom. It encourages you to trust your gut feelings and inner guidance, using your intuition to navigate complex situations and to make decisions that align with your true self.

Nurturing energy: This card also represents nurturing energy and the importance of self-care. It suggests that you take time to nurture yourself and to ensure that your emotional needs are met, allowing you to be a source of support for others.

NUMEROLOGICAL SIGNIFICANCE

The number thirteen associated with the Queen represents mastery, maturity, and the embodiment of the qualities of the suit. The Queen of Cups embodies these qualities and emphasizes the importance of emotional maturity and the mastery of intuitive insights.

Mastery: The energy of the Queen signifies mastery and the ability to navigate your emotions with wisdom and grace. The Queen of Cups encourages you to embrace your emotional intelligence and to use it to guide your interactions and decisions.

Maturity: The Queen also represents emotional maturity and the ability to offer compassionate support to others. The Queen of Cups reminds you to approach your relationships with understanding and empathy, using your maturity to foster deep connections.

Embodiment: The Queen highlights the embodiment of the qualities of the suit of Cups. The Queen of Cups encourages you to fully embrace your compassionate and intuitive nature, using it to nurture yourself and those around you.

The Queen of Cups is a card of emotional depth, compassion, and intuitive wisdom. It encourages you to embrace the energy of "heart wisdom" and to trust your emotional intelligence and intuitive insights. This card serves as a reminder to nurture your inner and outer worlds with love and compassion, to listen to your heart, and to use your intuitive guidance to navigate your life. Celebrate your empathetic nature, offer support and understanding to others, and ensure that your own emotional needs are met. By honoring your heart's wisdom, you can navigate complex situations with grace and create deep, meaningful connections with those around you.

QUEEN OF CUPS REVERSED

Emotional insecurity: Feeling vulnerable, lacking emotional stability and confidence. Build emotional resilience and self-compassion.

Codependency: Overreliance on others for emotional support, leading to imbalance. Cultivate independence and self-reliance.

Neglect: Ignoring your own emotional needs, self-sacrifice leading to burnout. Prioritize self-care and well-being.

King *of* Cups

MEANING IN A TAROT READING

When the King of Cups appears in a reading, it signifies emotional maturity, stability, and the mastery of one's emotions. This card embodies the energy of "emotional maturity," highlighting the importance of being in control of your feelings, offering compassionate leadership, and maintaining balance in emotional situations. It encourages you to navigate your emotions with wisdom and to use your emotional intelligence to guide and support others.

Emotional maturity: The mantra of this card, "Emotional maturity," emphasizes the importance of being in control of your emotions and responding to situations with wisdom and understanding. It suggests that you have reached a level of emotional stability that allows you to handle challenges with grace and compassion.

Stability: The King of Cups represents emotional stability and the ability to remain calm and composed in difficult situations. It encourages you to maintain balance in your emotional life and to provide a stabilizing presence for others.

Compassionate leadership: This card signifies compassionate leadership and the ability to offer guidance and support with empathy. It suggests that you use your emotional intelligence to lead others, creating an environment of trust and understanding.

Mastery of emotions: The King of Cups highlights the mastery of emotions and the importance of being in tune with your feelings. It encourages you to understand your emotional responses and to use this awareness to navigate complex situations effectively.

Supportive presence: This card also represents being a supportive presence for others. It suggests that you offer a listening ear and a compassionate heart to those who need it, using your emotional maturity to provide comfort and guidance.

NUMEROLOGICAL SIGNIFICANCE

The number fourteen associated with the King represents mastery, authority, and the culmination of the qualities of the suit. The King of Cups embodies these qualities and emphasizes the importance of emotional mastery and the ability to lead with empathy and compassion.

Mastery: The energy of the King signifies mastery and the ability to control and understand your emotions fully. The King of Cups encourages you to use your emotional intelligence to navigate your life and to help others do the same.

Authority: The King also represents authority and the ability to lead with confidence. The King of Cups reminds you that true leadership comes from understanding and compassion, and that emotional maturity is a powerful tool in guiding others.

Culmination: The King highlights the culmination of the qualities of the suit of Cups. The King of Cups encourages you to embody emotional stability, compassion, and wisdom, using these qualities to create a positive impact in your life and the lives of those around you.

The King of Cups is a card of emotional maturity, stability, and compassionate leadership. It encourages you to embrace the energy of "emotional maturity" and to use your emotional intelligence to guide and support others. This card serves as a reminder to maintain balance in your emotional life, to lead with empathy, and to offer a stabilizing presence in difficult situations. Celebrate your mastery of emotions, use your emotional intelligence to navigate complex situations, and provide compassionate leadership to those who need it. By embodying emotional maturity, you can create a positive and supportive environment for yourself and others.

KING OF CUPS REVERSED

Emotional manipulation: Using emotions to control or manipulate others, leading to conflict and mistrust. Practice honesty and integrity in relationships.

Volatility: Emotional instability, frequent mood swings causing tension. Work on emotional regulation and stability.

Detachment: Disconnection from feelings, avoiding emotional intimacy and vulnerability. Open up and allow yourself to connect emotionally.

THE SUIT OF SWORDS

Ace *of* Swords

MEANING IN A TAROT READING

When the Ace of Swords appears in a reading, it signifies the arrival of new ideas, mental clarity, and the power of intellect. This card embodies the energy of a "new idea," highlighting the importance of embracing fresh perspectives and innovative thinking. It encourages you to use your intellect and clarity of thought to cut through confusion and pursue new opportunities with determination and confidence.

New idea: The mantra of this card, "New idea," emphasizes the importance of embracing and acting upon fresh ideas and perspectives. It suggests that a breakthrough in your thinking or a new insight is on the horizon, offering you the clarity and direction you need.

Mental clarity: The Ace of Swords represents mental clarity and the ability to see things from a new perspective. It encourages you to cut through confusion and to approach situations with a clear and focused mind.

Intellectual power: This card signifies the power of intellect and the importance of using your mental abilities to solve problems and make decisions. It suggests that your intellect is a powerful tool that can help you navigate challenges and pursue new opportunities.

Truth and justice: The Ace of Swords highlights the importance of truth and justice. It encourages you to seek the truth in all situations and to stand up for what is right, using your clarity of thought to advocate for fairness and integrity.

New beginnings: This card also represents new beginnings and the potential for fresh starts. It suggests that new opportunities are available to you and that by embracing new ideas, you can initiate positive changes in your life.

NUMEROLOGICAL SIGNIFICANCE

In numerology, the Ace is associated with the number one, representing new beginnings, potential, and the start of a new cycle. The Ace of Swords, as the first card in the suit of Swords, embodies these qualities and emphasizes the importance of mental clarity and innovative thinking in initiating new beginnings.

New beginnings: The energy of the Ace signifies new beginnings and the potential for fresh starts. The Ace of Swords encourages you to embrace new ideas and to use your mental clarity to initiate positive changes.

Potential: The Ace also represents potential and the promise of what can be achieved through clear thinking and intellectual power. The Ace of Swords reminds you that your mind is a powerful tool that can help you unlock new opportunities.

Start of a new cycle: The Ace highlights the start of a new cycle and the importance of approaching this new phase with a clear and focused mind. The Ace of Swords encourages you to use your intellect and clarity of thought to navigate this new cycle successfully.

The Ace of Swords is a card of new ideas, mental clarity, and the power of intellect. It encourages you to embrace the energy of "new ideas" and to use your mental abilities to cut through confusion and to pursue new opportunities with determination and confidence. This card serves as a reminder to approach situations with a clear and focused mind, to seek the truth, and to stand up for what is right. By embracing new ideas and using your intellectual power, you can initiate positive changes and unlock new opportunities in your life. Celebrate the arrival of fresh perspectives and the potential for new beginnings and let your clarity of thought guide you toward success.

ACE OF SWORDS REVERSED

Confusion: Lack of clarity, mental fog, making it difficult to make decisions. Seek clarity through meditation and reflection.

Miscommunication: Messages misunderstood or not received, leading to misunderstandings and conflict. Strive for clear and effective communication.

Missed ideas: Failure to act on important thoughts or insights, leading to missed opportunities. Be attentive to your ideas and act on them.

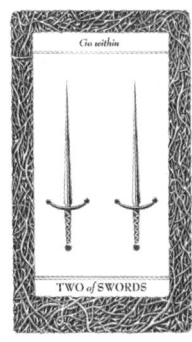

Two of Swords

MEANING IN A TAROT READING

When the Two of Swords appears in a reading, it signifies a moment of indecision, inner conflict, and the need for introspection. This card embodies the energy of "Go within," highlighting the importance of turning inward to find clarity and resolve inner conflicts. It encourages you to seek balance and to trust your intuition as you navigate difficult choices and uncertain situations.

Go within: The mantra of this card, "Go within," emphasizes the importance of introspection and inner reflection. It suggests that the answers you seek can be found within yourself and that by taking time to look inward, you can gain clarity and understanding.

Indecision: The Two of Swords represents a state of indecision and the difficulty of making a choice. It encourages you to pause and reflect, rather than rushing into a decision without considering all aspects.

Inner conflict: This card signifies inner conflict and the struggle between opposing forces or ideas. It suggests that you may be experiencing a mental or emotional stalemate, and it encourages you to explore these conflicts deeply.

Introspection: The Two of Swords highlights the importance of introspection and self-awareness. It encourages you to take time for inner reflection, to understand your true feelings and motivations, and to find a path that aligns with your inner truth.

Balance: This card also represents the need for balance and harmony. Finding equilibrium between opposing forces or ideas is key to resolving your inner conflicts and making informed decisions.

NUMEROLOGICAL SIGNIFICANCE

In numerology, the number two represents duality, balance, and partnership. The Two of Swords, as the second card in the suit of Swords, embodies these qualities and emphasizes the importance of finding balance and harmony through introspection and inner reflection.

Duality: The energy of the Two signifies duality and the presence of opposing forces or ideas. The Two of Swords encourages you to explore both sides of a situation and to seek a balanced perspective.

Balance: The Two also represents balance and the importance of finding harmony between conflicting forces. The Two of Swords reminds you that balance is essential for making clear and informed decisions.

Partnership: The Two highlights the significance of partnership and collaboration. The Two of Swords encourages you to seek guidance from others and to consider different viewpoints as you navigate your inner conflicts.

The Two of Swords is a card of indecision, inner conflict, and the need for introspection. It encourages you to embrace the energy of "Go within" and to seek clarity and understanding through inner reflection. This card serves as a reminder to pause and reflect, explore your inner conflicts, and find balance and harmony within yourself. By turning inward and trusting your intuition, you can navigate difficult choices and uncertain situations with greater clarity and confidence. Celebrate the process of introspection and the wisdom it brings, and let your inner truth guide you toward balance and resolution.

TWO OF SWORDS REVERSED

Decision made: Finally making a choice after a period of indecision, moving forward. Embrace your decision and take action.

Inner conflict: Continuing struggle despite outward resolution, feeling torn. Address internal conflicts to find peace.

Truth revealed: Hidden factors coming to light, forcing action and clarity. Accept the truth and adjust your plans accordingly.

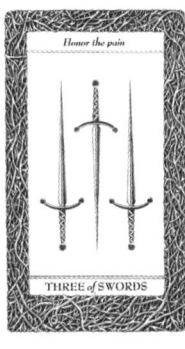

Three *of* Swords

MEANING IN A TAROT READING

When the Three of Swords appears in a reading, it signifies heartache, sorrow, and the experience of emotional pain. This card asks you to "Honor the pain," highlighting the importance of acknowledging and processing your emotions. It encourages you to confront your feelings of hurt and disappointment, allowing yourself to heal and grow from the experience.

Honor the pain: The mantra of this card, "Honor the pain," emphasizes the importance of acknowledging and accepting your emotional pain. It suggests that by confronting and embracing your feelings, you can begin the process of healing and transformation.

Heartache: The Three of Swords represents heartache and emotional pain. It encourages you to recognize and accept your feelings of sorrow, allowing yourself to experience and process them fully.

Sorrow: This card signifies sorrow and the impact of loss or betrayal. It suggests that you may be going through a difficult emotional period, and it encourages you to honor your feelings and give yourself time to heal.

Emotional healing: The Three of Swords highlights the importance of emotional healing. It encourages you to confront your pain, seek support if needed, and allow yourself the time and space to heal and recover.

Acceptance: This card also represents the process of acceptance. It suggests that by accepting your pain and the reality of your situation, you can find a path forward and begin to rebuild and renew your emotional strength.

NUMEROLOGICAL SIGNIFICANCE

In numerology, the number three represents growth, expansion, and the integration of different elements. The Three of Swords, as the third card in the suit of Swords, embodies these qualities and emphasizes the importance of emotional growth and the healing process.

Growth: The energy of the Three signifies growth and the potential for transformation through challenging experiences. The Three of Swords encourages you to see your pain as an opportunity for emotional growth and self-discovery.

Expansion: The Three also represents expansion and the integration of different emotional experiences. The Three of Swords reminds you that your heartache can lead to a deeper understanding of yourself and your emotions.

Integration: The Three highlights the importance of integrating your emotional experiences into your overall journey. The Three of Swords encourages you to honor your pain and to use it as a catalyst for personal growth and healing.

The Three of Swords is a card of heartache, sorrow, and emotional pain. It encourages you to embrace the energy of "Honor the pain" and to acknowledge and accept your feelings. This card serves as a reminder that by confronting and embracing your emotional pain, you can begin the process of healing and transformation. Allow yourself to fully experience and process your feelings, seek support if needed, and give yourself the time and space to heal. By honoring your pain, you can find a path forward, rebuild your emotional strength, and grow from the experience. Celebrate the process of emotional healing and the wisdom it brings, and let your pain guide you toward greater understanding and resilience.

THREE OF SWORDS REVERSED
Healing: Beginning to recover from heartbreak or betrayal, finding peace. Allow yourself to heal and move forward.

Forgiveness: Letting go of past pain, mending relationships and moving on. Practice forgiveness for yourself and others.

Lingering pain: Difficulty fully moving on, residual hurt and emotional scars. Continue the healing process and seek support if needed.

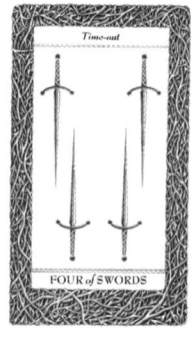

Four *of* Swords

MEANING IN A TAROT READING

When the Four of Swords appears in a reading, it signifies rest, recuperation, and the need for a break from stress or conflict. This card embodies the energy of "time-out," highlighting the importance of taking a step back to rest, reflect, and rejuvenate. It encourages you to honor your need for peace and quiet, allowing yourself the necessary time to recover and gain clarity.

Time-out: The mantra of this card, "Time-out," emphasizes the importance of taking a break and allowing yourself to rest. Stepping away from the hustle and bustle is necessary for your well-being and mental clarity.

Rest and recuperation: The Four of Swords represents a period of rest and recuperation. It encourages you to take a break from the demands of daily life to recharge your energy and regain your strength.

Reflection: This card signifies the need for quiet reflection and introspection. By taking time out to reflect, you can gain valuable insights and a clearer perspective on your situation.

Recovery: The Four of Swords highlights the importance of recovery, whether from illness, stress, or emotional turmoil. It encourages you to prioritize your health and well-being, allowing yourself the time to heal fully.

Peace and solitude: This card also represents the need for peace and solitude. Finding a quiet space where you can be alone with your thoughts is essential for restoring balance and harmony in your life.

NUMEROLOGICAL SIGNIFICANCE
In numerology, the number four represents stability, structure, and foundation. The Four of Swords, as the fourth card in the suit of Swords, embodies these qualities and emphasizes the importance of building a strong foundation for mental and emotional well-being through rest and reflection.

Stability: The energy of the Four signifies stability and the need to create a stable environment for rest and recuperation. The Four of Swords encourages you to establish a routine that allows for regular breaks and downtime.

Structure: The Four also represents structure and the importance of creating a supportive framework for your mental and emotional health. The Four of Swords reminds you to build a structure that supports your need for rest and reflection.

Foundation: The Four highlights the importance of establishing a strong foundation for your well-being. The Four of Swords encourages you to take time out to rest and reflect, ensuring that you have a solid foundation from which to navigate life's challenges.

The Four of Swords is a card of rest, recuperation, and the need for a break. It encourages you to embrace the energy of "time-out" and to prioritize your need for rest and reflection. This card serves as a reminder to take a step back from the demands of daily life, to find a quiet space for introspection, and to allow yourself the time to recover and rejuvenate. By honoring your need for peace and solitude, you can restore balance and harmony in your life, gain valuable insights, and build a strong foundation for mental and emotional well-being. Celebrate the importance of taking a time-out and letting yourself rest and reflect, knowing that this will lead to greater clarity and resilience.

FOUR OF SWORDS REVERSED

Restlessness: Inability to rest or relax, feeling the need for action. Find ways to balance rest and activity.

Recovery: Slowly coming out of a period of rest or illness, regaining strength. Continue to prioritize your health and well-being.

Burnout: Ignoring the need for rest, leading to exhaustion and fatigue. Recognize the signs of burnout and take steps to prevent it.

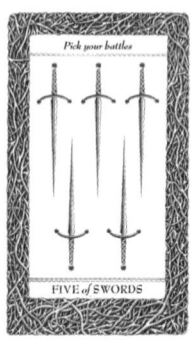

Five *of* Swords

MEANING IN A TAROT READING

When the Five of Swords appears in a reading, it signifies conflict, tension, and the consequences of battles won or lost. This card embodies the energy of "picking your battles," highlighting the importance of discerning which conflicts are worth engaging in and which are better avoided. It encourages you to consider the long-term impact of your actions and to seek resolution with wisdom and tact.

Pick your battles: The mantra of this card, "Pick your battles," emphasizes the importance of choosing your conflicts wisely. It suggests that not all battles are worth fighting and that careful consideration is needed to avoid unnecessary strife.

Conflict and tension: The Five of Swords represents conflict and tension, often resulting from disagreements or power struggles. It encourages you to recognize these conflicts' underlying causes and approach them with a clear mind.

Consequences: This card signifies the consequences of conflicts, whether they are victories or losses. It suggests that even when you win a battle, there may be negative repercussions that need to be considered.

Wisdom and tact: The Five of Swords highlights the importance of wisdom and tact in resolving conflicts. It encourages you to approach disagreements with a strategic mindset, aiming for resolution rather than escalation.

Self-reflection: This card also represents the need for self-reflection. It suggests that you examine your motives and actions in conflicts, understanding how they contribute to the situation and what lessons can be learned.

NUMEROLOGICAL SIGNIFICANCE

In numerology, the number five represents change, challenge, and the need for adaptability. The Five of Swords, as the fifth card in the suit of Swords, embodies these qualities and emphasizes the importance of navigating conflicts with adaptability and discernment.

Change: The energy of the Five signifies change and the challenges that come with it. The Five of Swords encourages you to adapt to changing circumstances and to choose your battles carefully.

Challenge: The Five also represents a challenge and the need to overcome obstacles. The Five of Swords reminds you that conflicts can be challenging but also offer opportunities for growth and learning.

Adaptability: The Five highlights the importance of adaptability in resolving conflicts. The Five of Swords encourages you to be flexible and to adjust your approach as needed to achieve the best outcomes.

The Five of Swords is a card of conflict, tension, and the consequences of battles won or lost. It encourages you to embrace the energy of "Pick your battles" and to choose your conflicts wisely. This card serves as a reminder to approach disagreements with wisdom and tact, to consider the long-term impact of your actions, and to seek resolution rather than escalation. You can navigate conflicts with greater clarity and effectiveness by discerning which battles are worth fighting and which are better avoided. Celebrate the lessons learned from conflicts and use your wisdom and adaptability to achieve positive outcomes and maintain harmony in your life.

FIVE OF SWORDS REVERSED

Resolution: Finding a way to end conflicts, seeking peace and reconciliation. Strive for harmony and understanding in relationships.

Regret: Feeling remorse over past actions or words, seeking forgiveness. Learn from past mistakes and make amends.

Avoidance: Evading confrontation, leading to unresolved issues and tension. Address conflicts directly to find resolution.

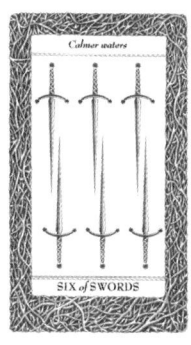

Six *of* Swords

MEANING IN A TAROT READING

When the Six of Swords appears in a reading, it signifies a journey toward recovery, transition, and moving away from difficulties. This card embodies the energy of "calmer waters," highlighting the importance of leaving behind turbulent situations and heading toward a more peaceful and stable environment. It encourages you to embrace change and trust that moving forward will bring relief and a new tranquility.

Calmer waters: The mantra of this card, "Calmer waters," emphasizes the importance of seeking peace and stability. It suggests that moving away from stressful or challenging situations will lead to a more serene and balanced state of being.

Transition: The Six of Swords represents a period of transition and change. It encourages you to embrace this journey, trusting that it will lead you to a better place both emotionally and mentally.

Recovery: This card signifies recovery from past difficulties and the beginning of a healing process. It suggests that by leaving behind what no longer serves you, you can start to heal and find peace.

Moving forward: The Six of Swords highlights the importance of moving forward and not dwelling on the past. It encourages you to focus on the future and the positive changes that lie ahead.

Guidance and support: This card also represents the support and guidance available to you during this transition. It suggests that you are not alone on this journey and that you have the assistance needed to navigate toward calmer waters.

NUMEROLOGICAL SIGNIFICANCE

In numerology, the number six represents harmony, balance, and the resolution of conflicts. The Six of Swords, as the sixth card in the suit of Swords, embodies these qualities and emphasizes the importance of finding peace and balance through transition and change.

Harmony: The energy of the Six signifies harmony and the resolution of conflicts. The Six of Swords encourages you to seek balance and peace as you transition from difficult situations to more-harmonious ones.

Balance: The Six also represents balance and the importance of creating a stable and peaceful environment. The Six of Swords reminds you that moving toward calmer waters will help restore balance in your life.

Resolution: The Six highlights the importance of resolving past conflicts and challenges. The Six of Swords encourages you to leave behind what no longer serves you and to focus on creating a peaceful and fulfilling future.

The Six of Swords is a card of recovery, transition, and moving toward a more peaceful state. It encourages you to embrace the energy of "calmer waters" and to seek peace and stability in your life. This card serves as a reminder that leaving behind turbulent situations and focusing on the future will lead to a more serene and balanced state of being. Trust in the journey, seek guidance and support, and embrace the positive changes that lie ahead. By moving forward and not dwelling on the past, you can find recovery and harmony in your life. Celebrate the transition toward calmer waters and the peace it brings, knowing that you are on the path to a better and more fulfilling future.

SIX OF SWORDS REVERSED

Stagnation: Difficulty moving on from a difficult situation, feeling stuck. Seek new perspectives and solutions to move forward.

Resistance: Refusal to change or adapt, staying stuck in old patterns. Embrace change and be open to new possibilities.

Returning troubles: Issues that were thought to be resolved are resurfacing, needing attention. Address unresolved issues to find lasting peace.

Seven *of* Swords

MEANING IN A TAROT READING

When the Seven of Swords appears in a reading, it signifies deception, betrayal, and the need for caution. This card embodies the energy of "deception," highlighting the importance of being aware of hidden motives and dishonesty from others or within yourself. It encourages you to stay vigilant, protect your interests, and act with integrity to navigate through tricky situations.

Deception: The mantra of this card, "Deception," emphasizes the importance of recognizing and dealing with dishonesty. It suggests that deception may be at play, either from others or within yourself, and urges you to address it head on.

Betrayal: The Seven of Swords represents betrayal and the feeling of being wronged. It encourages you to be cautious and protect yourself from those acting against your interests.

Caution: This card signifies the need for caution and careful planning. It suggests that you should be strategic in your actions, keeping your plans and intentions guarded to avoid potential pitfalls.

Hidden motives: The Seven of Swords highlights the presence of hidden motives and agendas. It encourages you to be mindful of the intentions of others and to ensure that your own actions are transparent and honest.

Self-deception: This card also represents self-deception and the potential for self-sabotage. It suggests that you examine your own actions and motives to ensure that you are not deceiving yourself or acting against your own best interests.

NUMEROLOGICAL SIGNIFICANCE

In numerology, seven represents introspection, analysis, and the quest for truth. The Seven of Swords, as the seventh card in the suit of Swords, embodies these qualities and emphasizes the importance of seeking truth and clarity amid deception and dishonesty.

Introspection: The energy of the Seven signifies introspection and the importance of looking within to understand hidden motives. The Seven of Swords encourages you to reflect on your own actions and the actions of others to uncover the truth.

Analysis: The Seven also represents analysis and the need for careful evaluation. The Seven of Swords reminds you to analyze situations thoroughly and be strategic to avoid deception.

Quest for truth: The Seven highlights the quest for truth and the importance of uncovering hidden agendas. The Seven of Swords encourages you to seek clarity and to ensure that your actions align with your true intentions and values.

The Seven of Swords is a card of deception, betrayal, and the need for caution. It encourages you to embrace the energy of "deception" and to stay vigilant against dishonesty, whether from others or within yourself. This card serves as a reminder to be cautious, protect your interests, and act with integrity. By being mindful of hidden motives and agendas, you can navigate tricky situations with greater clarity and confidence. Reflect on your own actions, seek the truth, and ensure that your intentions are transparent and honest. Celebrate the awareness and wisdom that come from recognizing and addressing deception, and use this knowledge to protect yourself and act with integrity.

SEVEN OF SWORDS REVERSED

Confession: Coming clean about past deceit or misdeeds, seeking redemption. Practice honesty and transparency.

Caught out: Deception being discovered, facing consequences and accountability. Accept responsibility and learn from your mistakes.

Honesty: Choosing to act with integrity, avoiding dishonest behavior. Build trust through honesty and ethical behavior.

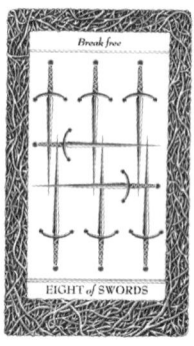

Eight *of* Swords

MEANING IN A TAROT READING

When the Eight of Swords appears in a reading, it signifies feelings of restriction, limitation, and the perception of being trapped. This card embodies the energy of "Break free," highlighting the importance of recognizing and overcoming self-imposed limitations and mental blocks. It encourages you to find the courage and clarity to liberate yourself from constraints and to take proactive steps toward freedom and empowerment.

Break free: The mantra of this card, "Break free," emphasizes the importance of recognizing and overcoming self-imposed limitations. It suggests that you have the power to liberate yourself from restrictive situations and mental blocks.

Restriction: The Eight of Swords represents a sense of restriction and feeling trapped. It encourages you to identify the areas in your life where you feel limited and to seek ways to break free from these constraints.

Limitation: This card signifies the perception of limitation and the belief that you are powerless. It suggests that these limitations may be more mental than physical, and encourages you to challenge these beliefs and seek solutions.

Self-imposed constraints: The Eight of Swords highlights self-imposed constraints and the impact of negative thinking. It encourages you to examine your thought patterns and to recognize how they may be contributing to your feelings of entrapment.

Courage and clarity: This card also represents the need for courage and clarity. By gaining a clear perspective and finding the inner strength to confront your fears, you can break free from limitations and move toward greater freedom.

NUMEROLOGICAL SIGNIFICANCE

In numerology, the number eight represents power, strength, and transformation. The Eight of Swords, as the eighth card in the suit of Swords, embodies these qualities and emphasizes the importance of using your inner strength to overcome limitations and achieve personal transformation.

Power: The energy of the Eight signifies personal power and the ability to take control of your situation. The Eight of Swords encourages you to recognize your inner strength and to use it to break free from constraints.

Strength: The Eight also represents strength and the courage to confront challenges. The Eight of Swords reminds you that you have the resilience to overcome obstacles and to liberate yourself from limiting beliefs.

Transformation: The Eight highlights the potential for transformation through breaking free from limitations. The Eight of Swords encourages you to seek change and embrace the opportunities for growth and empowerment that come from overcoming constraints.

The Eight of Swords is a card of restriction, limitation, and the perception of being trapped. It encourages you to embrace the energy of "Break free" and to recognize and overcome self-imposed limitations. This card serves as a reminder that you have the power and strength to liberate yourself from restrictive situations and mental blocks. By gaining clarity, challenging negative thought patterns, and finding the courage to confront your fears, you can break free from constraints and move toward greater freedom and empowerment. Celebrate your inner strength and the transformative power of breaking free and use this knowledge to create a more fulfilling and liberated life.

EIGHT OF SWORDS REVERSED

Liberation: Breaking free from mental constraints or limitations, finding freedom. Embrace your newfound freedom and move forward with confidence.

Clarity: Seeing a way out of a difficult situation, gaining insight. Use this clarity to make informed decisions.

Empowerment: Taking control of your own destiny, overcoming fear and doubt. Empower yourself to achieve your goals.

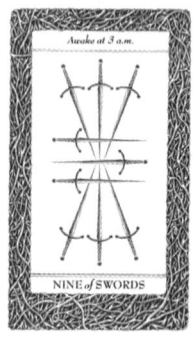

Nine *of* Swords

MEANING IN A TAROT READING

When the Nine of Swords appears in a reading, it signifies anxiety, worry, and sleepless nights. This card embodies the energy of "awake at 3 a.m.," highlighting the importance of acknowledging your fears and finding ways to address them. It encourages you to confront the sources of your anxiety, seek support, and take steps toward healing and peace of mind.

Awake at 3 a.m.: The mantra of this card, "Awake at 3 a.m.," emphasizes the restless nights and persistent worries that keep you awake. It suggests that your mind is preoccupied with anxieties that need to be addressed and resolved.

Anxiety: The Nine of Swords represents feelings of anxiety and worry. It encourages you to recognize these feelings and to seek ways to manage and reduce your stress.

Worry: This card signifies a period of intense worry and mental anguish. It suggests that you may be overwhelmed by negative thoughts and fears, and it encourages you to find ways to alleviate these burdens.

Sleepless nights: The Nine of Swords highlights the impact of anxiety on your sleep and overall well-being. It encourages you to address the underlying issues causing your sleepless nights, and to seek rest.

Facing fears: This card also represents the need to face your fears and confront the sources of your anxiety. By acknowledging and addressing your worries, you can begin to find peace and clarity.

NUMEROLOGICAL SIGNIFICANCE

In numerology, the number nine represents completion, attainment, and the culmination of a cycle. The Nine of Swords, as the ninth card in the suit of Swords, embodies these qualities and emphasizes the importance of addressing your anxieties to achieve mental and emotional resolution.

Completion: The energy of the Nine signifies the culmination of a cycle and the need to address lingering issues. The Nine of Swords encourages you to confront your anxieties to find closure and peace of mind.

Attainment: The Nine also represents attainment and the ability to overcome challenges. The Nine of Swords reminds us that facing our fears can help us achieve a sense of resolution and move toward a calmer state of being.

Culmination: The Nine highlights the culmination of your worries and the importance of addressing them to move forward. The Nine of Swords encourages you to seek solutions and to work toward resolving your anxieties.

The Nine of Swords is a card of anxiety, worry, and sleepless nights. It encourages you to embrace the energy of "awake at 3 a.m." and to acknowledge the fears and anxieties that keep you awake. This card serves as a reminder to confront the sources of your worry, seek support, and take steps toward healing and peace of mind. By addressing your anxieties and finding ways to manage your stress, you can achieve a sense of resolution and move toward a calmer and more restful state. Celebrate your strength in facing your fears and use this knowledge to create a more peaceful and balanced life.

NINE OF SWORDS REVERSED

Relief: Finding solace from anxiety or nightmares, gaining peace. Allow yourself to relax and find comfort.

Facing fears: Confronting and dealing with sources of worry and stress. Address your fears head on, to find resolution.

Hope: Renewed optimism, seeing light at the end of the tunnel, finding hope. Focus on the positive and keep moving forward.

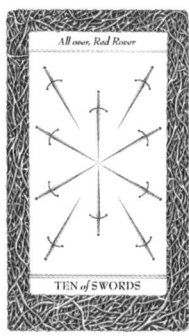

Ten *of* Swords

MEANING IN A TAROT READING

When the Ten of Swords appears in a reading, it signifies the end of a difficult situation, a betrayal, or a painful conclusion. This card embodies the energy of "All over, Red Rover," highlighting the finality of a challenging phase and the need to accept and move on. It encourages you to acknowledge the end, let go of what no longer serves you, and embrace the opportunity for a new beginning.

All over, Red Rover: The mantra of this card, "All over, Red Rover," emphasizes the end of a difficult situation. It suggests that a significant chapter in your life is ending, and it is time to accept this ending and move forward.

End of a difficult situation: The Ten of Swords represents the conclusion of a challenging phase or the end of a struggle. It encourages you to recognize that the worst is over and to focus on healing and recovery.

Betrayal: This card signifies feelings of betrayal or being let down by others. It suggests that you may have experienced a painful ending due to someone else's actions, and it encourages you to process these emotions and find a way to move on.

Painful conclusion: The Ten of Swords highlights the pain and difficulty associated with endings. It acknowledges that while endings can be painful, they are also a necessary part of life's cycles, paving the way for new beginnings.

Acceptance and letting go: This card also represents the importance of acceptance and letting go. It encourages you to release what no longer serves you and to embrace the opportunity for renewal and transformation.

NUMEROLOGICAL SIGNIFICANCE

In numerology, ten represents completion, finality, and the beginning of a new cycle. The Ten of Swords, as the tenth card in the suit of Swords, embodies these qualities and emphasizes the importance of accepting endings and preparing for new beginnings.

Completion: The energy of the Ten signifies the completion of a cycle and the end of a difficult phase. The Ten of Swords encourages you to acknowledge this ending and to focus on the opportunities that lie ahead.

Finality: The Ten also represents finality and the definitive conclusion of a situation. The Ten of Swords reminds you that some things must come to an end to make way for new growth and transformation.

New beginnings: The Ten highlights the potential for new beginnings following an ending. The Ten of Swords encourages you to embrace the renewal opportunity and prepare for a fresh start.

The Ten of Swords is a card of endings, betrayal, and painful conclusions. It encourages you to embrace the energy of "All over, Red Rover" and to accept the end of a difficult situation. This card serves as a reminder that while endings can be painful, they are also a necessary part of life's cycles, paving the way for new beginnings. By acknowledging the end, letting go of what no longer serves you, and focusing on healing and recovery, you can prepare for a fresh start and new opportunities.

Celebrate the completion of a challenging phase and the potential for future renewal and transformation.

TEN OF SWORDS REVERSED

Recovery: Beginning to heal from a painful ending or betrayal, finding strength. Allow yourself time to heal and rebuild.

Regeneration: Finding strength after a crisis, rebuilding and moving forward. Use your experiences to grow and become stronger.

Survival: Overcoming the worst, learning from hardship, gaining resilience. Recognize your resilience and celebrate your survival.

Page *of* Swords

MEANING IN A TAROT READING

When the Page of Swords appears in a reading, it signifies curiosity, mental agility, and a thirst for knowledge. The mantra "Use your head" highlights the importance of thinking critically, being observant, and approaching situations clearly and analytically. It encourages you to embrace your intellectual curiosity and to use your mental acuity to navigate challenges and uncover the truth.

Use your head: This card's mantra, "Use your head," emphasizes the importance of thinking logically and critically. It suggests approaching situations with a clear and analytical mind, using your intellect to find solutions and gain insights.

Curiosity: The Page of Swords represents a strong desire to learn and understand. It encourages you to embrace your curiosity and to seek out new information and experiences that stimulate your mind.

Mental agility: This card signifies mental agility and the ability to think quickly and adapt to changing circumstances. It suggests that you use your sharp mind to navigate challenges and to stay one step ahead.

Observation: The Page of Swords highlights the importance of being observant and paying attention to details. It encourages you to watch and listen carefully, using your keen perception to uncover the truth and gain a deeper understanding of your situation.

Communication: This card also represents clear and effective communication. It suggests that you express your thoughts and ideas confidently and clearly and that you engage in honest and open dialogue with others.

NUMEROLOGICAL SIGNIFICANCE

The number eleven associated with the Page represents beginnings, potential, and a youthful approach. The Page of Swords embodies these qualities and emphasizes the importance of intellectual curiosity and the pursuit of knowledge.

Beginnings: The energy of the Page signifies new beginnings and the start of a journey toward greater understanding. The Page of Swords encourages you to embrace new ideas and approach learning with enthusiasm and curiosity.

Potential: The Page also represents potential and the promise of intellectual growth. The Page of Swords reminds you that by using your head and thinking critically, you can unlock new opportunities and achieve your goals.

Youthful approach: The Page highlights the importance of a youthful approach to learning and problem-solving. The Page of Swords encourages you to stay curious, open minded, and eager to explore new ideas and perspectives.

The Page of Swords is a card of curiosity, mental agility, and the pursuit of knowledge. It encourages you to embrace the energy of "Use your head" and to approach situations with a clear and analytical mind. This card serves as a reminder to think critically, be observant, and communicate effectively. By embracing your intellectual curiosity and using your mental acuity, you can navigate challenges, uncover the truth, and achieve your goals. Celebrate your curiosity and the potential for intellectual growth and let your keen mind guide you toward greater understanding and success.

PAGE OF SWORDS REVERSED

Gossip: Engaging in or being affected by harmful rumors and talk. Avoid gossip and focus on truthful communication.

Impulsiveness: Acting without thought, leading to mistakes and misunderstandings. Think before you act to avoid unnecessary conflicts.

Deception: Misleading others, or being misled, leading to confusion. Strive for honesty and clarity in your interactions.

Knight *of* Swords

MEANING IN A TAROT READING

When the Knight of Swords appears in a reading, it signifies swift action, determination, and the pursuit of goals with unwavering focus. This card embodies the energy of "forging forward," highlighting the importance of moving decisively and with purpose. It encourages you to act quickly, stay focused on your objectives, and use your intellect and willpower to overcome obstacles and succeed.

Forging forward: The mantra of this card, "Forging forward," emphasizes the importance of taking decisive action and moving forward with determination. It suggests that now is the time to confidently and quickly act on your goals and ambitions.

Swift action: The Knight of Swords represents swift action and the ability to move quickly toward your goals. It encourages you to seize opportunities and to act decisively to achieve your objectives.

Determination: This card signifies strong determination and the willpower to overcome obstacles. Stay focused on your goals and push through any challenges with persistence and resolve.

Focus and clarity: The Knight of Swords highlights the importance of maintaining focus and clarity in your pursuits. It encourages you to keep your mind sharp and to use your intellect to navigate through complex situations and make informed decisions.

Courage and boldness: This card also represents courage and boldness. It suggests that you embrace a fearless approach to pursuing your dreams and that you are willing to take risks to achieve success.

NUMEROLOGICAL SIGNIFICANCE

The number twelve associated with the Knight represents action, movement, and the pursuit of goals. The Knight of Swords embodies these qualities and emphasizes the importance of taking swift and decisive action to achieve your ambitions.

Action: The energy of the Knight signifies action and the need to move forward with purpose. The Knight of Swords encourages you to take decisive steps toward your goals and to act with confidence and determination.

Movement: The Knight also represents movement and the drive to pursue your ambitions. The Knight of Swords reminds you to stay focused on your path and to keep pushing forward, no matter the obstacles.

Pursuit of goals: The Knight highlights the importance of pursuing your goals with unwavering focus and determination. The Knight of Swords encourages you to stay committed to your ambitions and to use your intellect and willpower to achieve success.

The Knight of Swords is a card of swift action, determination, and the pursuit of goals. It encourages you to embrace the energy of "forging forward" and to move decisively toward your objectives. This card serves as a reminder to act quickly, stay focused, and use your intellect and willpower to overcome obstacles and achieve success. By maintaining clarity and determination, you can navigate challenges and achieve your ambitions with confidence.

Celebrate your courage and boldness and let your decisive actions propel you toward your goals and dreams.

KNIGHT OF SWORDS REVERSED

Recklessness: Acting rashly, without considering consequences, leading to conflict. Slow down and consider the long-term impact of your actions.

Aggression: Overly confrontational, leading to unnecessary conflicts and tension. Practice patience and diplomacy.

Impatience: Rushing into things, lack of planning and foresight, causing issues. Take time to plan and prepare before taking action.

Queen *of* Swords

MEANING IN A TAROT READING

When the Queen of Swords appears in a reading, it signifies clarity, truth, and the ability to cut through confusion to get to the heart of the matter. This card embodies the energy of "the heart of the matter," highlighting the importance of honesty, clear communication, and intellectual discernment. It encourages you to approach situations with a sharp mind and a keen sense of perception, allowing you to see things as they truly are and to make decisions that are based on truth and logic.

The heart of the matter: The mantra of this card, "The heart of the matter," emphasizes the importance of seeking truth and clarity. It suggests that you focus on understanding the core issues in any situation, cutting through any distractions or deceptions.

Clarity: The Queen of Swords represents mental clarity and the ability to see things as they truly are. It encourages you to use your intellect and sharp perception to gain a clear understanding of your circumstances.

Truth: This card signifies a commitment to truth and honesty. It suggests that you value transparency and that you are willing to confront difficult truths to resolve issues and make informed decisions.

Clear communication: The Queen of Swords highlights the importance of clear and direct communication. It encourages you to express your thoughts and ideas with precision and confidence, ensuring that your message is understood.

Intellectual discernment: This card also represents intellectual discernment and the ability to make logical and well-reasoned decisions. It suggests that you rely on your critical-thinking skills to navigate complex situations and separate fact from fiction.

NUMEROLOGICAL SIGNIFICANCE

The number thirteen associated with the Queen represents mastery, maturity, and the embodiment of the qualities of the suit. The Queen of Swords embodies these qualities and emphasizes the importance of intellectual mastery and the pursuit of truth and clarity.

Mastery: The energy of the Queen signifies mastery and the ability to navigate complex situations easily. The Queen of Swords encourages you to use your intellectual skills and sharp perception to achieve clarity and resolve issues.

Maturity: The Queen also represents maturity and the ability to approach situations with wisdom and experience. The Queen of Swords reminds you to rely on your knowledge and understanding to make well-informed decisions.

Embodiment: The Queen highlights the embodiment of the qualities of the suit of Swords. The Queen of Swords encourages you to fully embrace your intellectual and communicative abilities, using them to seek truth and clarity in all areas of your life.

The Queen of Swords is a card of clarity, truth, and intellectual discernment. It encourages you to embrace the energy of "the heart of the matter" and to focus on seeking truth and clarity in all situations. This card serves as a reminder to use your intellect and sharp perception to cut through confusion and to approach situations with honesty and clear communication. By seeking the heart of the matter, you can gain a deeper understanding of your circumstances and make well-informed decisions that are based on truth and logic. Celebrate your intellectual mastery and the pursuit of clarity and let your keen mind guide you toward greater understanding and resolution.

QUEEN OF SWORDS REVERSED

Coldness: Emotionally distant or harsh, lacking compassion and empathy. Practice empathy and understanding in your relationships.

Manipulation: Using intellect to deceive or control others, leading to mistrust. Be honest and ethical in your interactions.

Judgmental: Critical and unforgiving, quick to judge others harshly. Practice forgiveness and understanding.

King *of* Swords

MEANING IN A TAROT READING

When the King of Swords appears in a reading, it signifies authority, intellectual power, and the ability to lead with truth and integrity. This card embodies the energy of "Lead with truth," highlighting the importance of using logic, honesty, and clear judgment in your actions and decisions. It encourages you to approach situations with fairness, to communicate effectively, and to lead with a strong moral compass.

Lead with truth: The mantra of this card, "Lead with truth," emphasizes the importance of guiding your actions and decisions with honesty and integrity. It suggests that true leadership comes from a place of truth and fairness.

Authority: The King of Swords represents authority and the ability to make decisive and well-reasoned decisions. It encourages you to take charge of your situations confidently and use your intellectual power to lead effectively.

Intellectual power: This card signifies intellectual strength and the capacity to think critically and analytically. It suggests that you use your sharp mind to navigate complex issues and to find solutions that are based on logic and reason.

Clear judgment: The King of Swords highlights the importance of clear judgment and the ability to see things objectively. It encourages you to evaluate situations without bias and to make decisions that are fair and just.

Honesty and integrity: This card also represents the values of honesty and integrity. It suggests that you lead by example, demonstrating truthfulness and ethical behavior in all your actions and interactions.

NUMEROLOGICAL SIGNIFICANCE

The number fourteen here represents mastery, completion, and the embodiment of the qualities of the suit. The King of Swords embodies these qualities and emphasizes the importance of intellectual mastery and leading with truth and integrity.

Mastery: The energy of the King signifies mastery and the ability to lead with confidence and authority. The King of Swords encourages you to use your intellectual skills and clear judgment to guide others and to make well-informed decisions.

Completion: The King also represents the culmination of the qualities of the suit of Swords. The King of Swords reminds you that true leadership is achieved through a deep understanding of truth, logic, and ethical principles.

Embodiment: The King highlights the embodiment of the qualities of the suit of Swords. The King of Swords encourages you to fully embrace your intellectual and communicative abilities, using them to lead with integrity and to uphold the values of truth and fairness.

The King of Swords is a card of authority, intellectual power, and the ability to lead with truth and integrity. It encourages you to embrace the energy of "Lead with truth" and to guide your actions and decisions with honesty and clear judgment. This card serves as a reminder to use your intellectual strength and objective thinking to navigate complex situations and to lead with fairness and ethical principles. By leading with truth, you can inspire confidence and respect and create a positive impact in your life and the lives of those around you. Celebrate your intellectual mastery and the values of honesty and integrity and let your clear judgment guide you toward effective leadership and meaningful accomplishments.

KING OF SWORDS REVERSED

Abuse of power: Using authority in a corrupt or unjust manner, causing harm. Lead with integrity and fairness.

Cruelty: Being harsh or ruthless, lacking empathy and compassion. Practice kindness and understanding.

Stubbornness: Refusing to listen to others, rigid and inflexible thinking. Be open to new ideas and perspectives.

THE SUIT OF PENTACLES

Ace *of* Pentacles

MEANING IN A TAROT READING
When the Ace of Pentacles appears in a reading, it signifies new beginnings, opportunities, and potential in material and financial matters. This card embodies the energy of "the new start," highlighting the importance of embracing new ventures, investments, and practical pursuits. It encourages you to recognize and seize opportunities leading to growth, abundance, and stability.

The new start: This card's mantra, "The new start," emphasizes the significance of new beginnings and opportunities. It suggests that you are at the threshold of a new venture or phase in your life that holds the potential for growth and prosperity.

Opportunities: The Ace of Pentacles represents fresh opportunities, particularly in the areas of career, finances, and material well-being. It encourages you to be open to new possibilities and to take advantage of opportunities that come your way.

Potential for growth: This card signifies the potential for growth and the promise of future success. It suggests that by investing your time, energy, and resources wisely, you can cultivate abundance and achieve your goals.

Material and financial stability: The Ace of Pentacles highlights the importance of material and financial stability. It encourages you to focus on building a solid foundation that can support your long-term ambitions and provide security.

Practicality and realism: This card also represents practicality and a grounded approach to new ventures. It suggests that you approach opportunities with a realistic mindset, considering the practical steps needed to achieve your desired outcomes.

NUMEROLOGICAL SIGNIFICANCE

In numerology, the Ace is associated with the number one, representing new beginnings, potential, and the start of a new cycle. The Ace of Pentacles, as the first card in the suit of Pentacles, embodies these qualities and emphasizes the importance of seizing new opportunities and laying the groundwork for future success.

New beginnings: The energy of the Ace signifies new beginnings and the potential for fresh starts. The Ace of Pentacles encourages you to embrace new opportunities and to take the first steps toward building a prosperous future.

Potential: The Ace also represents potential and the promise of what can be achieved through diligent effort and wise investments. The Ace of Pentacles reminds you that by recognizing and seizing opportunities, you can unlock new levels of success and abundance.

Start of a new cycle: The Ace highlights the start of a new cycle and the importance of laying a strong foundation. The Ace of Pentacles encourages you to approach new ventures with a practical mindset and to focus on creating stability and growth.

The Ace of Pentacles is a card of new beginnings, opportunities, and potential in the material and financial realms. It encourages you to embrace the energy of "the new start" and to recognize and seize opportunities that can lead to growth and prosperity. This card serves as a reminder to focus on building a solid foundation, to approach new ventures with practicality and realism, and to invest your time and resources wisely. By embracing new opportunities and laying the groundwork for future success, you can cultivate abundance and achieve your goals. Celebrate the promise of new beginnings and growth potential and let your practical approach guide you toward a prosperous and fulfilling future.

ACE OF PENTACLES REVERSED

Missed opportunity: Failure to capitalize on new beginnings or offers, leading to regret. Be attentive to opportunities and act on them.

Financial loss: Potential for monetary setbacks or bad investments, causing stress. Manage your finances carefully and avoid risky investments.

Instability: Lack of security or groundedness in endeavors, leading to anxiety. Focus on building a stable foundation for your goals.

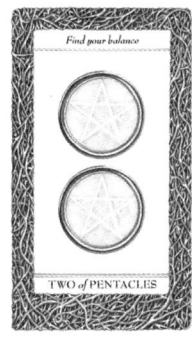

Two of Pentacles

MEANING IN A TAROT READING

When the Two of Pentacles appears in a reading, it signifies balance, adaptability, and the ability to manage multiple priorities. This card embodies the energy of "Find your balance," highlighting the importance of juggling responsibilities and maintaining equilibrium in your life. It encourages you to stay flexible, to prioritize effectively, and to find harmony amid the various demands on your time and energy.

Find your balance: The mantra of this card, "Find your balance," emphasizes the need to maintain equilibrium while managing multiple tasks and responsibilities. It suggests that you focus on finding a rhythm that allows you to handle your commitments effectively.

Adaptability: The Two of Pentacles represents adaptability and the ability to adjust to changing circumstances. It encourages you to remain flexible and to be open to new approaches in managing your responsibilities.

Juggling priorities: This card signifies the act of juggling multiple priorities and responsibilities. It suggests that you develop skills in time management and organization to keep everything running smoothly.

Harmony and equilibrium: The Two of Pentacles highlights the importance of harmony and equilibrium in your life. It encourages you to seek balance in all areas, ensuring that you do not neglect any aspect of your well-being.

Financial management: This card also represents the need for careful financial management and the ability to balance your income and expenses. It suggests that you pay attention to your finances and make informed decisions to maintain stability.

NUMEROLOGICAL SIGNIFICANCE

In numerology, the number two represents duality, balance, and partnership. The Two of Pentacles, as the second card in the suit of Pentacles, embodies these qualities and emphasizes the importance of finding balance and harmony in managing your responsibilities and resources.

Duality: The energy of the Two signifies duality and the presence of multiple elements that need to be balanced. The Two of Pentacles encourages you to harmonize different aspects of your life and to manage your priorities effectively.

Balance: The Two also represents balance and the importance of maintaining equilibrium. The Two of Pentacles reminds you that finding balance is essential for managing your responsibilities and achieving stability.

Partnership: The Two highlights the significance of partnership and collaboration. The Two of Pentacles encourages you to seek support and to work together with others to achieve your goals.

The Two of Pentacles is a card of balance, adaptability, and the ability to manage multiple priorities. It encourages you to embrace the energy of "Find your balance" and to stay flexible and adaptable in managing your responsibilities. This card serves as a reminder to prioritize effectively, to seek harmony and equilibrium in all areas of your life, and to develop skills in time management and organization. By finding your balance and staying adaptable, you can navigate the demands on your time and energy with greater ease and effectiveness. Celebrate the importance of balance and harmony and let your flexibility and adaptability guide you toward a more balanced and fulfilling life.

TWO OF PENTACLES REVERSED

Imbalance: Struggling to juggle responsibilities, feeling overwhelmed and stressed. Prioritize tasks and manage your time effectively.

Disorganization: Lack of order, leading to mistakes, delays, and frustration. Create a structured plan to stay organized.

Financial strain: Difficulty managing resources effectively, leading to financial stress. Budget carefully and seek financial advice if needed.

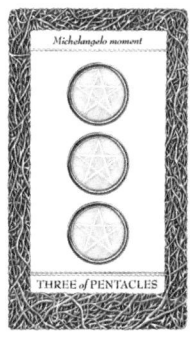

Three *of* Pentacles

MEANING IN A TAROT READING

When the Three of Pentacles appears in a reading, it signifies collaboration, teamwork, and the pursuit of excellence in your work and creative endeavors. This card embodies the energy of the "Michelangelo moment," highlighting the importance of working with others while also recognizing that this is your path and your legacy. It encourages you to embrace collaboration and strive for mastery and craftsmanship in all that you do.

Michelangelo moment: This card's mantra, "Michelangelo moment," emphasizes the significance of creating something enduring and magnificent by leaving a lasting legacy through collaboration and dedicated effort.

Collaboration: The Three of Pentacles represents the value of working with others to achieve a common goal. It encourages you to embrace teamwork and to recognize the strengths and contributions of your collaborators.

Teamwork: This card signifies the power of teamwork and the collective effort required to accomplish great things. It suggests that by working together harmoniously, you can achieve more than you could alone.

Pursuit of excellence: The Three of Pentacles highlights the importance of striving for excellence and mastery in your work. It encourages you to dedicate yourself to your craft and to take pride in the quality and precision of your efforts.

Recognition: This card also represents the recognition and appreciation of your skills and contributions. It suggests that your hard work and dedication will be acknowledged and valued by others.

NUMEROLOGICAL SIGNIFICANCE

In numerology, the number three represents growth, creativity, and collaboration. The Three of Pentacles, as the third card in the suit of Pentacles, embodies these qualities and emphasizes the importance of working with others to achieve growth and excellence.

Growth: The energy of the Three signifies growth and the potential for expansion through collaboration. The Three of Pentacles encourages you to embrace opportunities for learning and development in your work.

Creativity: The Three also represents creativity and the expression of your unique talents. The Three of Pentacles reminds you that collaboration can enhance your creative efforts and lead to innovative and inspired results.

Collaboration: The Three highlights the significance of working with others to achieve shared goals. The Three of Pentacles encourages you to value the contributions of your collaborators and to work together toward a common vision.

The Three of Pentacles is a card of collaboration, teamwork, and the pursuit of excellence. It encourages you to embrace the energy of the "Michelangelo moment" and to recognize that even in partnership, this is your path and your legacy. This card serves as a reminder to work harmoniously with others, to strive for mastery and craftsmanship in your work, and to take pride in your contributions. By embracing teamwork and dedicating yourself to excellence, you can create something enduring and magnificent that reflects your unique talents and vision. Celebrate the power of collaboration and the pursuit of excellence and let your efforts leave a legacy.

THREE OF PENTACLES REVERSED

Lack of collaboration: Issues working with others, teamwork problems causing delays. Foster open communication and cooperation in group projects.

Mediocrity: Subpar performance, not meeting expectations or standards. Strive for excellence and continual improvement.

Criticism: Facing judgment or disapproval for your work, causing demotivation. Accept constructive feedback and use it to improve.

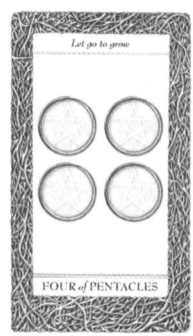

Four *of* Pentacles

MEANING IN A TAROT READING

When the Four of Pentacles appears in a reading, it signifies holding on tightly to resources, possessions, or control, often leading to a sense of security but also potential stagnation. This card embodies the energy of "Let go to grow," highlighting the importance of releasing the need for control and allowing for growth and new opportunities. It encourages you to examine what you are holding on to too tightly and to consider the benefits of letting go to make space for new possibilities.

Let go to grow: The mantra of this card, "Let go to grow," emphasizes the need to release control and possessions to allow for growth and expansion. It suggests that clinging too tightly to what you have can prevent you from experiencing new opportunities and progress.

Security and control: The Four of Pentacles represents a desire for security and control over one's resources and environment. It encourages you to recognize the balance between maintaining security and being open to change and growth.

Possessiveness: This card signifies possessiveness and the fear of loss. It suggests that you may be holding on to your possessions, finances, or relationships too tightly, which can lead to a sense of stagnation.

Stagnation: The Four of Pentacles highlights the potential for stagnation when you are unwilling to let go. It encourages you to consider how your desire for control and security may be holding you back from new opportunities and experiences.

Financial caution: This card also represents financial caution and the importance of managing your resources wisely. It suggests that while it is important to be prudent with your finances, it is equally important to be open to investing in new opportunities that can lead to growth.

NUMEROLOGICAL SIGNIFICANCE

In numerology, the number four represents stability, structure, and foundation. The Four of Pentacles, as the fourth card in the suit of Pentacles, embodies these qualities and emphasizes the importance of balancing security with openness to growth and change.

Stability: The energy of the Four signifies stability and the desire to create a secure and structured environment. The Four of Pentacles encourages you to build a solid foundation while remaining open to new possibilities.

Structure: The Four also represents structure and the importance of having a stable framework in place. The Four of Pentacles reminds you that while structure is important, flexibility is also necessary for growth.

Foundation: The Four highlights the significance of a strong foundation for financial and personal well-being. The Four of Pentacles encourages you to balance maintaining this foundation with being open to growth and new opportunities.

The Four of Pentacles is a card of security, control, and the potential for stagnation. It encourages you to embrace the energy of "Let go to grow" and to recognize the importance of releasing control and possessions to allow for growth and expansion. This card serves as a reminder to balance your desire for security with openness to change and new opportunities. By letting go of what you are holding on to too tightly, you can make space for growth and progress in your life. Celebrate the stability and structure you have created, and let your willingness to let go guide you toward new experiences and opportunities for growth.

FOUR OF PENTACLES REVERSED

Greed: Holding on too tightly to possessions, fear of loss causing anxiety. Practice generosity and let go of material attachments.

Release: Letting go of material attachments or control, finding freedom. Embrace the freedom that comes from releasing what no longer serves you.

Instability: Financial or emotional insecurity, lack of stability causing stress. Focus on creating a stable and secure environment.

Five *of* Pentacles

MEANING IN A TAROT READING

When the Five of Pentacles appears in a reading, it signifies hardship, financial struggles, and feelings of being left out or isolated. This card embodies the energy of "on the outside," highlighting the experience of exclusion, loss, or feeling disconnected from support and resources. It encourages you to seek assistance, remain hopeful, and recognize that this challenging period is temporary and can lead to growth and resilience.

On the outside: The mantra of this card, "On the outside," emphasizes feelings of exclusion, hardship, and being disconnected from support. It suggests that you may be going through a difficult time where you feel isolated or left out.

Hardship: The Five of Pentacles represents hardship and financial struggles. It encourages you to acknowledge the difficulties you are facing and to seek practical solutions to overcome them.

Isolation: This card signifies feelings of isolation and being excluded from a sense of community or support. Reaching out for help and connecting with others can provide much-needed relief and assistance.

Hope and resilience: The Five of Pentacles highlights the importance of maintaining hope and resilience during tough times. It encourages you to keep faith that these challenges are temporary and that you have the strength to overcome them.

Seeking assistance: This card also represents the need to seek assistance and support. It suggests that there are resources and help available to you, and that reaching out to others can make a significant difference in your situation.

NUMEROLOGICAL SIGNIFICANCE

In numerology, the number five represents change, challenge, and instability. The Five of Pentacles, as the fifth card in the suit of Pentacles, embodies these qualities and emphasizes the importance of navigating through change and hardship with resilience and hope.

Change: The energy of the Five signifies change and the challenges that come with it. The Five of Pentacles encourages you to adapt to changing circumstances and to find ways to overcome the difficulties you are facing.

Challenge: The Five also represents challenges and the need to confront and address obstacles. The Five of Pentacles reminds you that while this period may be challenging, it is also an opportunity for growth and resilience.

Instability: The Five highlights the instability that can accompany periods of hardship. The Five of Pentacles encourages you to seek stability and support, recognizing that this instability is temporary and can lead to greater strength and understanding.

The Five of Pentacles is a card of hardship, financial struggles, and feelings of being left out or isolated. It encourages you to embrace the energy of "on the outside," and to acknowledge the challenges you are facing. This card serves as a reminder to seek assistance, maintain hope, and recognize that this difficult period is temporary. By reaching out for support, staying resilient, and finding practical solutions, you can overcome these challenges and emerge stronger. Celebrate your strength and resilience and let your hope guide you through this period of hardship toward a more stable and connected future.

FIVE OF PENTACLES REVERSED

Recovery: Beginning to find solutions to financial or emotional hardship, finding hope. Seek support and take proactive steps to improve your situation.

Hope: Seeing a way out of difficult circumstances, finding optimism. Focus on the positive and believe in your ability to overcome challenges.

Assistance: Receiving help or support when needed, finding relief and support. Be open to accepting help from others.

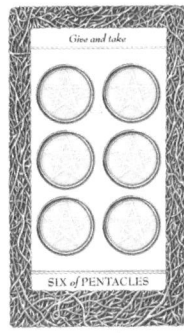

Six *of* Pentacles

MEANING IN A TAROT READING

When the Six of Pentacles appears in a reading, it signifies generosity, balance, and the importance of giving and receiving. This card embodies the energy of "give and take," highlighting the reciprocal nature of relationships and the flow of resources. It encourages you to embrace generosity, seek balance in your interactions, and understand that true prosperity comes both from giving and receiving support.

Give and take: The mantra of this card, "Give and take," emphasizes the importance of balance and reciprocity in relationships and financial matters. It suggests that both generosity and receiving support are crucial for a healthy, prosperous life.

Generosity: The Six of Pentacles represents acts of generosity and kindness. It encourages you to share your resources, time, and support with those in need, recognizing that generosity enriches both the giver and the receiver.

Receiving support: This card signifies the importance of being open to receiving help and support from others. It suggests that accepting assistance is as important as giving it, and that doing so creates a balanced and harmonious flow of energy.

Balance: The Six of Pentacles highlights the need for balance in all areas of life. It encourages you to find equilibrium in your finances, relationships, and personal interactions, ensuring that giving and receiving are in harmony.

Prosperity: This card also represents the prosperity that comes from balanced and generous interactions. It suggests that true wealth is found not only in material possessions but also in the quality of your relationships and the willingness to share and receive support.

NUMEROLOGICAL SIGNIFICANCE

In numerology, the number six represents harmony, balance, and responsibility. The Six of Pentacles, as the sixth card in the suit of Pentacles, embodies these qualities and emphasizes the importance of generosity and balance in achieving prosperity and well-being.

Harmony: The energy of the Six signifies harmony and the need to create balance in your life. The Six of Pentacles encourages you to seek harmony in your relationships and financial matters, ensuring that giving and receiving are balanced.

Balance: The Six also represents balance and the importance of maintaining equilibrium. The Six of Pentacles reminds you that true prosperity comes from a balanced approach to giving and receiving support.

Responsibility: The Six highlights the responsibility that comes with prosperity and the importance of using your resources wisely. The Six of Pentacles encourages you to share your abundance with others and to be open to receiving help when needed.

The Six of Pentacles is a card of generosity, balance, and the reciprocal nature of giving and receiving. It encourages you to embrace the energy of "give and take" and to seek harmony in your relationships and financial matters. This card serves as a reminder to be generous with your resources, to accept support graciously, and to recognize the prosperity that comes from balanced interactions. By creating a harmonious flow of giving and receiving, you can achieve greater well-being and enrich your life and the lives of those around you. Celebrate the importance of generosity and balance and let your actions reflect the beauty of reciprocal support and shared prosperity.

SIX OF PENTACLES REVERSED

Imbalance: Unequal give and take, either giving too much or too little, causing tension. Strive for balance in your relationships and interactions.

Selfishness: Withholding help or resources from others, leading to conflict. Practice generosity and consider the needs of others.

Debt: Financial obligations becoming burdensome, causing stress. Manage your finances carefully and avoid unnecessary debt.

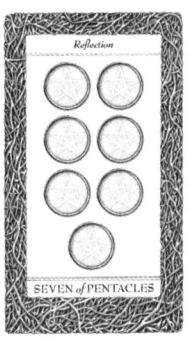

Seven *of* Pentacles

MEANING IN A TAROT READING

When the Seven of Pentacles appears in a reading, it signifies reflection, assessment, and patience. This card embodies the energy of "reflection," highlighting the importance of evaluating your progress and considering your next steps. It encourages you to take a step back, review your efforts, and determine whether you are on the right path or if adjustments are needed to achieve your long-term goals.

Reflection: The mantra of this card, "Reflection," emphasizes the importance of taking time to evaluate your progress and to reflect on your efforts and outcomes. It suggests that careful assessment is needed before moving forward.

Assessment: The Seven of Pentacles represents the process of assessing your work and investments. It encourages you to review your progress, understand what is working well, and identify areas that may need improvement.

Patience: This card signifies the need for patience and the understanding that growth and success take time. It suggests that while you may not see immediate results, your continued efforts will eventually bear fruit.

Evaluation: The Seven of Pentacles highlights the importance of evaluating your goals and strategies. It encourages you to consider whether your current approach aligns with your long-term objectives, and to make necessary adjustments.

Long-term planning: This card also represents the value of long-term planning and the benefits of thinking ahead. It suggests that by reflecting on your progress and planning carefully, you can achieve sustainable success and growth.

NUMEROLOGICAL SIGNIFICANCE

The number seven represents introspection, analysis, and the quest for understanding. The Seven of Pentacles, as the seventh card in the suit of Pentacles, embodies these qualities and emphasizes the importance of reflection and thoughtful assessment in achieving your goals.

Introspection: The energy of the Seven signifies introspection and the need to look within to understand your progress and goals. The Seven of Pentacles encourages you to take time for self-reflection and to evaluate your efforts.

Analysis: The Seven also represents analysis and the importance of carefully assessing your work. The Seven of Pentacles reminds you to analyze your progress and to use this understanding to guide your future actions.

Quest for understanding: The Seven highlights the quest for understanding and the importance of gaining insights from your experiences. The Seven of Pentacles encourages you to seek deeper understanding and to apply this knowledge to your long-term planning.

The Seven of Pentacles is a card of reflection, assessment, and patience. It encourages you to embrace the energy of "reflection" and to take time to evaluate your progress and efforts. This card serves as a reminder to review your work, understand what is working, and identify areas for improvement. You can achieve sustainable success and growth by thoughtfully reflecting on your progress and planning. Celebrate the importance of introspection and analysis and let your careful assessment guide you toward achieving your long-term goals with patience and understanding.

SEVEN OF PENTACLES REVERSED

Impatience: Wanting results too quickly, lack of patience causing frustration. Practice patience and trust the process.

Lack of reward: Efforts not yielding expected returns, causing disappointment. Reevaluate your goals and strategies to find more-effective approaches.

Frustration: Feeling stuck or unfulfilled with progress, causing demotivation. Stay focused on your long-term goals and keep moving forward.

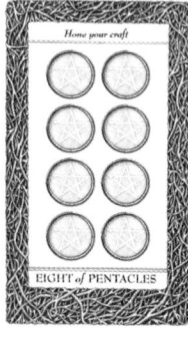

Eight *of* Pentacles

MEANING IN A TAROT READING

When the Eight of Pentacles appears in a reading, it signifies hard work, dedication, and the pursuit of mastery. This card embodies the energy of "Hone your craft," highlighting the importance of dedicating yourself to refining your skills and achieving excellence. It encourages you to focus on your work, embrace continual improvement, and strive for perfection in all that you do.

Hone your craft: The mantra of this card, "Hone your craft," emphasizes the importance of refining and perfecting your skills through dedicated practice. It suggests that focused effort and commitment are essential to achieving mastery and success.

Dedication: The Eight of Pentacles represents dedication and commitment to your work. It encourages you to invest time and energy into developing your talents and achieving your goals.

Mastery: This card signifies the pursuit of mastery and the continual improvement of your skills. It suggests that you focus on refining your craft and striving for excellence in all your endeavors.

Focus and diligence: The Eight of Pentacles highlights the importance of focus and diligence. It encourages you to concentrate on your tasks, pay attention to detail, and maintain a high standard of quality in your work.

Continual improvement: This card also represents the value of continual improvement and learning. By embracing a mindset of growth and development, you can achieve greater success and fulfillment.

NUMEROLOGICAL SIGNIFICANCE

In numerology, the number eight represents power, strength, and transformation. The Eight of Pentacles, as the eighth card in the suit of Pentacles, embodies these qualities and emphasizes the importance of using your inner strength to achieve mastery and transformation through hard work and dedication.

Power: The energy of the Eight signifies personal power and the ability to take control of your growth and development. The Eight of Pentacles encourages you to harness your inner strength to achieve mastery in your chosen field.

Strength: The Eight also represents strength and resilience in the face of challenges. The Eight of Pentacles reminds you that through hard work and dedication, you can overcome obstacles and achieve your goals.

Transformation: The Eight highlights the potential for transformation through continual improvement. The Eight of Pentacles encourages you to break free from old patterns and to embrace a mindset of growth and development.

The Eight of Pentacles is a card of hard work, dedication, and the pursuit of mastery. It encourages you to embrace the energy of "Hone your craft" and to commit to continual improvement and the diligent practice required to refine your skills and achieve your goals. This card serves as a reminder to focus on your work, embrace a growth mindset, and strive for excellence in all that you do. By honing your craft and dedicating yourself to mastery, you can achieve greater success and transformation. Celebrate the power of hard work and dedication and let your commitment to continual improvement guide you toward achieving your aspirations.

EIGHT OF PENTACLES REVERSED

Perfectionism: Overly critical of your work, never satisfied, leading to stress. Practice self-compassion and celebrate your progress.

Laziness: Lack of effort or dedication to tasks, causing stagnation. Find motivation and discipline to stay committed to your goals.

Skill development: Neglecting to improve or hone your abilities, causing setbacks. Invest in learning and personal growth.

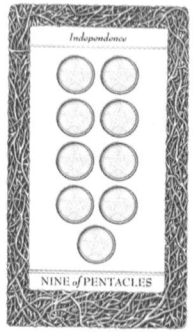

Nine *of* Pentacles

MEANING IN A TAROT READING

When the Nine of Pentacles appears in a reading, it signifies self-sufficiency, abundance, and the rewards of hard work. This card embodies the energy of "independence," highlighting the importance of achieving personal success and enjoying the fruits of your labor. It encourages you to appreciate your accomplishments, embrace your autonomy, and take pride in your self-reliance.

Independence: The mantra of this card, "Independence," emphasizes the importance of self-sufficiency and personal achievement. It suggests that you take pride in your ability to stand on your own and to enjoy the rewards of your hard work.

Self-sufficiency: The Nine of Pentacles represents self-sufficiency and the ability to provide for yourself. It encourages you to recognize and celebrate your independence and the success you have achieved through your efforts.

Abundance: This card signifies abundance and the enjoyment of material comforts. It suggests that you take time to appreciate the wealth and prosperity you have created in your life.

Rewards of hard work: The Nine of Pentacles highlights the rewards that come from dedication and hard work. It encourages you to acknowledge and enjoy the benefits of your efforts and to take pride in your accomplishments.

Autonomy: This card also represents autonomy and the freedom that comes from being self-reliant. It suggests that you embrace your independence and the confidence that comes with knowing you can rely on yourself.

NUMEROLOGICAL SIGNIFICANCE

In numerology, the number nine represents completion, fulfillment, and attainment. The Nine of Pentacles, as the ninth card in the suit of Pentacles, embodies these qualities and emphasizes the importance of achieving personal success and enjoying the fruits of your labor.

Completion: The energy of the Nine signifies completion and the culmination of your efforts. The Nine of Pentacles encourages you to recognize the completion of a significant phase and to celebrate your achievements.

Fulfillment: The Nine also represents fulfillment and the satisfaction that comes from achieving your goals. The Nine of Pentacles reminds you to enjoy the sense of fulfillment that comes from your hard work and dedication.

Attainment: The Nine highlights the attainment of personal success and the rewards of your efforts. The Nine of Pentacles encourages you to take pride in your accomplishments and to appreciate the abundance you have created.

The Nine of Pentacles is a card of self-sufficiency, abundance, and the rewards of hard work. It encourages you to embrace the energy of "independence" and to take pride in your achievements and self-reliance. This card serves as a reminder to appreciate the wealth and prosperity you have created, to enjoy the rewards of your efforts, and to celebrate your autonomy and self-sufficiency. By recognizing and appreciating your accomplishments, you can experience a sense of fulfillment and satisfaction from knowing you have achieved success through your own efforts. Celebrate your independence and the abundance you have created, and let your self-reliance guide you toward continued success and fulfillment.

NINE OF PENTACLES REVERSED

Overindulgence: Excessive focus on luxury or materialism, leading to emptiness. Find balance and focus on what truly brings you joy.

Dependency: Relying too much on others for financial support, causing insecurity. Cultivate independence and self-sufficiency.

Setbacks: Facing obstacles in achieving self-sufficiency, causing frustration. Stay resilient and find solutions to overcome challenges.

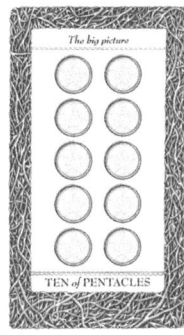

Ten *of* Pentacles

MEANING IN A TAROT READING

When the Ten of Pentacles appears in a reading, it signifies wealth, legacy, and long-term success. This card embodies the energy of "the big picture," highlighting the importance of looking beyond immediate gains and focusing on long-term stability and prosperity. It encourages you to consider the broader impact of your actions, build a legacy, and appreciate the interconnectedness of family, tradition, and wealth.

The big picture: The mantra of this card, "The big picture," emphasizes the importance of long-term thinking and planning. It suggests that you focus on creating lasting success and stability that will benefit future generations.

Wealth and prosperity: The Ten of Pentacles represents significant wealth and financial stability. It encourages you to recognize and appreciate the abundance you have created and to use it wisely for the benefit of yourself and others.

Legacy: This card signifies the creation of a lasting legacy. Your efforts and achievements will have a long-term impact, benefiting not only you but also your family and future generations.

Long-term success: The Ten of Pentacles highlights the importance of long-term success and the benefits of strategic planning. It encourages you to think beyond immediate gains and to focus on sustainable growth and stability.

Family and tradition: This card also represents the importance of family and tradition. It suggests that your success is intertwined with the support and values of your family, and it encourages you to honor and maintain these connections.

NUMEROLOGICAL SIGNIFICANCE

In numerology, the number ten represents completion, fulfillment, and the start of a new cycle. The Ten of Pentacles, as the tenth card in the suit of Pentacles, embodies these qualities and emphasizes the importance of achieving long-term success and creating a legacy.

Completion: The energy of the Ten signifies the completion of a significant phase and the achievement of long-term goals. The Ten of Pentacles encourages you to recognize the culmination of your efforts and to celebrate your successes.

Fulfillment: The Ten also represents fulfillment and the satisfaction that comes from achieving long-term stability and prosperity. The Ten of Pentacles reminds you to appreciate the sense of fulfillment that comes from building a legacy.

New cycle: The Ten highlights the start of a new cycle, emphasizing the importance of planning for the future and creating sustainable success. The Ten of Pentacles encourages you to focus on long-term growth and the impact of your actions on future generations.

The Ten of Pentacles is a card of wealth, legacy, and long-term success. It encourages you to embrace the energy of "the big picture" and to focus on creating lasting stability and prosperity. This card serves as a reminder to consider the broader impact of your actions, to build a legacy that will benefit future generations, and to appreciate the interconnectedness of family, tradition, and wealth. You can achieve sustainable growth and fulfillment by focusing on long-term success and strategic planning. Celebrate the wealth and prosperity you have created and let your commitment to the big picture guide you toward continued success and a lasting legacy.

TEN OF PENTACLES REVERSED

Conflict: Disputes within the family or regarding inheritance, causing tension. Address conflicts with empathy and understanding.

Instability: Lack of financial security, threats to legacy, causing anxiety. Focus on creating a stable and secure foundation.

Loss: Potential for significant financial or material loss, causing stress. Be proactive in protecting your assets and resources.

Page *of* Pentacles

MEANING IN A TAROT READING

When the Page of Pentacles appears in a reading, it signifies new opportunities, curiosity, and a keen interest in learning and development, particularly in practical and material matters. This card embodies the energy of "curious exploration," highlighting the importance of approaching your goals and ambitions with a sense of curiosity and a willingness to learn. It encourages you to explore new ventures, study diligently, and remain open to the possibilities that lie ahead.

Curious exploration: The mantra of this card, "Curious exploration," emphasizes the importance of approaching life and its opportunities with a sense of curiosity and eagerness to learn. It suggests that you remain open to new experiences and discoveries.

New opportunities: The Page of Pentacles represents the beginning of new ventures or projects, especially those related to career, education, or personal development. It encourages you to seize new opportunities and to explore potential paths for growth.

Learning and development: This card signifies a strong desire to learn and grow. It suggests that you dedicate yourself to studying, acquiring new skills, and developing your talents in practical and tangible ways.

Practical approach: The Page of Pentacles highlights the importance of a practical and grounded approach to your goals. It encourages you to focus on realistic and achievable steps, ensuring that your efforts lead to tangible results.

Diligence: This card also represents diligence and the value of hard work. It suggests that by applying yourself with dedication and perseverance, you can achieve your ambitions and build a solid foundation for future success.

NUMEROLOGICAL SIGNIFICANCE

The Page is associated with the number eleven, representing new beginnings, potential, and a youthful approach. The Page of Pentacles, as the first card in the court cards of the suit of Pentacles, embodies these qualities and emphasizes the importance of practical exploration and diligent effort.

New beginnings: The energy of the Page signifies new beginnings and the potential for practical and material growth. The Page of Pentacles encourages you to embrace new opportunities for learning and development.

Potential: The Page also represents potential and the promise of what can be achieved through curiosity and diligent effort. The Page of Pentacles reminds you that by exploring new ventures and applying yourself, you can unlock new levels of success.

Youthful approach: The Page highlights the importance of maintaining a youthful approach to learning and exploration. The Page of Pentacles encourages you to stay curious and open minded as you pursue your goals.

The Page of Pentacles is a card of new opportunities, curiosity, and practical exploration. It encourages you to embrace the energy of "curious exploration" and to approach your goals with a sense of curiosity and a willingness to learn. This card serves as a reminder to seize new opportunities, dedicate yourself to learning and development, and apply a practical and grounded approach to your ambitions. By embracing new experiences and maintaining a diligent effort, you can achieve tangible results and build a solid foundation for future success. Celebrate the joy of curious exploration and let your practical efforts guide you toward new and fulfilling achievements.

PAGE OF PENTACLES REVERSED

Procrastination: Delaying action, not following through on plans, causing setbacks. Take initiative and stay committed to your goals.

Lack of focus: Difficulty concentrating or committing to goals, causing frustration. Create a clear plan and stay focused on your objectives.

Missed opportunities: Overlooking chances for growth or learning, causing regret. Stay attentive and seize opportunities when they arise.

Knight *of* Pentacles

MEANING IN A TAROT READING

When the Knight of Pentacles appears in a reading, it signifies dedication, focus, and a methodical approach to achieving goals. This card embodies the energy of "dedication and focus," highlighting the importance of steady and consistent effort in pursuing your ambitions. It encourages you to remain committed to your path, to work diligently, and to maintain a disciplined and practical approach in all your endeavors.

Dedication and focus: The mantra of this card, "Dedication and focus," emphasizes the importance of staying committed and focused on your goals. Consistent effort and determination are key to achieving success.

Steady progress: The Knight of Pentacles represents steady and reliable progress. It encourages you to take a methodical approach to your tasks, ensuring that each step is carefully planned and executed.

Methodical approach: This card signifies a practical and disciplined approach to achieving your ambitions. It suggests that you focus on the details and maintain a clear and structured plan to reach your goals.

Reliability: The Knight of Pentacles highlights the importance of being reliable and dependable. It encourages you to build a reputation for being trustworthy and consistent in your efforts.

Hard work: This card also represents the value of hard work and perseverance. It suggests that by dedicating yourself to your tasks and maintaining focus, you can achieve long-term success and stability.

NUMEROLOGICAL SIGNIFICANCE

The Knight is associated with the number twelve, representing growth, progress, and the pursuit of goals with determination. The Knight of Pentacles, as a court card in the suit of Pentacles, embodies these qualities and emphasizes the importance of dedication and focus in achieving practical and material success.

Growth: The energy of the Knight signifies growth and the continual pursuit of progress. The Knight of Pentacles encourages you to remain focused on your goals and to work steadily toward achieving them.

Progress: The Knight also represents progress and the importance of moving forward with determination. The Knight of Pentacles reminds you that consistent effort and dedication are essential for long-term success.

Determination: The Knight highlights the significance of determination and perseverance. The Knight of Pentacles encourages you to stay committed to your path and to maintain a disciplined approach to your tasks.

The Knight of Pentacles is a card of dedication, focus, and steady progress. It encourages you to embrace the energy of "dedication and focus" and to remain committed to your goals with a methodical and disciplined approach. This card serves as a reminder to take a practical and structured approach to your tasks, focus on the details, and maintain consistent effort in all your endeavors. By staying dedicated and focused, you can achieve long-term success and build a solid foundation for the future. Celebrate the value of hard work and perseverance and let your disciplined efforts guide you toward achieving your ambitions with reliability and determination.

KNIGHT OF PENTACLES REVERSED

Stubbornness: Resistance to change, unwilling to adapt, causing stagnation. Be open to new ideas and approaches.

Laziness: Lack of motivation, avoiding responsibilities, causing delays. Find motivation and discipline to stay committed to your tasks.

Perfectionism: Overly meticulous, causing delays and frustration. Practice flexibility and adapt to changing circumstances.

Queen *of* Pentacles

MEANING IN A TAROT READING

When the Queen of Pentacles appears in a reading, it signifies nurturing, practicality, and a strong connection to the material world. This card embodies the energy of being "grounded," highlighting the importance of staying connected to reality, managing resources wisely, and providing care and support to others. It encourages you to embrace a balanced and nurturing approach to your responsibilities and to cultivate a sense of stability and security.

Grounded: The mantra of this card, "Grounded," emphasizes the importance of staying connected to the earth and maintaining a practical approach to life. It suggests that you focus on building stability and managing your resources wisely.

Nurturing: The Queen of Pentacles represents a nurturing and caring energy. It encourages you to provide support and care to those around you, creating a harmonious and nurturing environment.

Practicality: This card signifies a practical and realistic approach to managing your responsibilities. Focus on practical solutions and take a sensible approach to your tasks and challenges.

Resource management: The Queen of Pentacles highlights the importance of managing resources wisely. It encourages you to be mindful of your finances, time, and energy, ensuring that you use them effectively to create stability and abundance.

Stability and security: This card also represents stability and security. By staying grounded and maintaining a practical approach, you can create a secure and stable foundation for yourself and your loved ones.

NUMEROLOGICAL SIGNIFICANCE

The Queen is associated with the number thirteen, representing transformation, nurturing, and the ability to create and maintain stability. The Queen of Pentacles, as a court card in the suit of Pentacles, embodies these qualities and emphasizes the importance of being grounded and practical in achieving material and emotional well-being.

Transformation: The energy of the Queen signifies transformation and the ability to create positive change through nurturing and practical efforts. The Queen of Pentacles encourages you to transform your environment into a nurturing and stable space.

Nurturing: The Queen also represents the nurturing aspect of life, highlighting the importance of providing care and support to others. The Queen of Pentacles reminds you to embrace your nurturing qualities and to create a harmonious and supportive environment.

Stability: The Queen highlights the significance of stability and security. The Queen of Pentacles encourages you to focus on building a stable foundation and to manage your resources effectively to ensure long-term stability.

The Queen of Pentacles is a card of nurturing, practicality, and groundedness. It encourages you to embrace the energy of being "grounded" and to maintain a practical and realistic approach to life. This card serves as a reminder to provide care and support to others, to manage your resources wisely, and to create a stable and secure environment. You can achieve material and emotional well-being by staying grounded and focusing on practical solutions. Celebrate the importance of nurturing and stability and let your practical efforts guide you toward creating a harmonious and abundant life.

QUEEN OF PENTACLES REVERSED

Neglect: Ignoring personal needs or the needs of loved ones, causing imbalance. Prioritize self-care and nurturing relationships.

Materialism: Overemphasis on wealth and possessions, causing emptiness. Focus on meaningful experiences and connections.

Dependency: Relying too much on others for support, causing insecurity. Cultivate independence and self-reliance.

King *of* Pentacles

MEANING IN A TAROT READING

When the King of Pentacles appears in a reading, it signifies wealth, stability, and the mastery of material and financial matters. This card embodies the energy of "structural power," highlighting the importance of building a strong and stable foundation, managing resources effectively, and exercising leadership with wisdom and confidence. It encourages you to take control of your material world, lead with authority, and create lasting prosperity.

Structural power: The mantra of this card, "Structural power," emphasizes the importance of building and maintaining a solid structure in all aspects of life. It suggests that you focus on creating stability, managing resources wisely, and exercising strong leadership.

Wealth and prosperity: The King of Pentacles represents significant wealth and financial stability. It encourages you to take control of your finances, make wise investments, and create long-term prosperity.

Leadership: This card signifies strong leadership and effectively managing people and resources. It suggests that you lead with authority and confidence, using your wisdom and experience to guide others.

Stability: The King of Pentacles highlights the importance of stability and security. It encourages you to build a solid foundation in your personal and professional life, ensuring long-term success and stability.

Practical wisdom: This card also represents practical wisdom and the ability to make sound decisions. It suggests that you use your practical knowledge and experience to navigate challenges and achieve your goals.

NUMEROLOGICAL SIGNIFICANCE

The King is associated with the number fourteen, representing mastery, authority, and the culmination of the suit's qualities. The King of Pentacles, as a court card in the suit of Pentacles, embodies these qualities and emphasizes the importance of structural power and stability in achieving long-term success.

Mastery: The energy of the King signifies mastery and the culmination of the qualities of the suit of Pentacles. The King of Pentacles encourages you to master your material world and to achieve a high level of competence and control.

Authority: The King also represents authority and the ability to lead confidently and wisely. The King of Pentacles reminds you to exercise your leadership skills and to guide others with a strong and steady hand.

Culmination: The King highlights the culmination of efforts and the achievement of long-term goals. The King of Pentacles encourages you to recognize and celebrate the success and stability you have built.

The King of Pentacles is a card of wealth, stability, and mastery of material and financial matters. It encourages you to embrace the energy of "structural power" and to focus on building and maintaining a solid foundation in all aspects of your life. This card serves as a reminder to take control of your finances, lead with authority and confidence, and create lasting prosperity through wise management and practical wisdom. By exercising strong leadership and focusing on stability, you can achieve long-term success and security. Celebrate the importance of structural power and let your practical efforts guide you toward creating a prosperous and stable life.

KING OF PENTACLES REVERSED

Greed: Overly focused on wealth and material gain, causing imbalance. Practice generosity and focus on what truly matters.

Corruption: Using power and resources unethically, causing harm. Lead with integrity and fairness.

Stagnation: Lack of growth or development, becoming complacent and stuck. Embrace change and seek continual improvement.

THREE TAROT SPREADS USING
Lieselle's Eternal Tarot

The relationship you develop with your Tarot deck is incredibly personal. The deck is not meant to intimidate you but to pique your curiosity. This way, when asking questions, a journey can unfold. You can use this deck in any way you see fit. I invite you to pick a random card and say the first thing that pops into your head. Trust that.

A Tarot spread is a specified format in which Tarot readings can be given. Many spreads exist on the basis of the questions asked or the situation being explored.

Here are some ways to engage with this deck:

1. Relationship Spread

Card 1: Your current state in the relationship

Card 2: Your partner's current state in the relationship

Card 3: The dynamics between you

Card 4: Potential challenges

Card 5: Advice for improvement

Card 6: Likely outcome

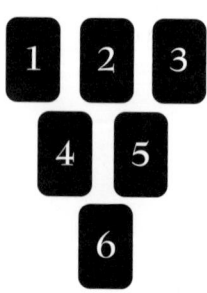

2. Focus of the Day

Card 1: What is the main focus for today?

Card 2: What should I be aware of?

Card 3: What action should I take?

Card 4: What is the underlying energy?

Card 5: What is the potential outcome for today?

3. Career/Finance Spread

Card 1: Your current financial/career situation

Card 2: Challenges you are facing

Card 3: Opportunities available to you

Card 4: What should you focus on?

Card 5: Advice for moving forward

Card 6: Likely outcome

By using these spreads, you can explore different aspects of your life, from relationships and daily insights to career and financial decisions. Each reading is an opportunity to connect with your intuition, gain deeper understanding, and navigate your journey with clarity and confidence.

Tarot reading is about interpreting the cards and connecting with your inner self and intuition. As you work with this deck, allow your intuition to guide you. The cards are tools to help you access deeper insights and understand the energies at play in your life. Trust your inner voice and let it lead you to the answers you seek.

Acknowledgments

We deeply appreciate the artists, Tarot readers, writers, and designers who paved the way for us. Their insights, vision, and inspiration have been instrumental in bringing this deck to life.

Bibliography

We found the following resources invaluable during our research:

Dean, Liz. *The Ultimate Guide to the Tarot*. Beverly, MA: Fair Winds, 2015.

McElroy, Mark. *A Guide to Tarot Card Meanings*. TarotTools, 2014.